ASIAN SAUCES
& MARINADES

ASIAN SAUCES & MARINADES

WENDY SWEETSER

FIREFLY BOOKS

A FIREFLY BOOK

Published by Firefly Books Ltd., 2002

First Printing
National Library Cataloguing in Publication Data

Sweetser, Wendy
Asian Sauces and Marinades

Includes index.

ISBN 1-55297-614-9

1. Sauces. 2. Marinades. 3. Cookery, Asian. I. Title.

TX819.A1S94 2002   641.8'14'095   C2002-900214-1

Publisher Cataloging-in-Publication Data (U.S.)

Sweetser, Wendy.
Asian Sauces and Marinades / Wendy Sweetser. – 1st ed.
[144] p. : col. photos. ;   cm.
Includes index.
Summary: A collection of 80 recipes for sauces, dips, glazes, braises and marinades.
Also includes background information on ingredients and accompanying dishes.
ISBN 1-55297-614-9 (pbk.)
1. Cookery—Asia. 2. Cookery (Sauces). I. Title.
641.5/ 95 21 CIP TX724.5.A1S94 2002

Published in Canada in 2002 by
Firefly Books Ltd.
3680 Victoria Park Avenue
Toronto, Ontario M2H 3K1

Published in the United States in 2002 by
Firefly Books (U.S.) Inc.
P.O. Box 1338, Ellicott Station
Buffalo, New York 14205

This book was designed and produced by
Quintet Publishing Limited
6 Blundell Street
London N7 9BH

OSM

Project Editor: Corinne Masciocchi
Editor: Anna Bennett
Art Director/Design: Simon Daley
Photographer: Iain Bagwell
Home Economist: Kathryn Hawkins
Creative Director: Richard Dewing
Publisher: Oliver Salzmann

Color separation in Hong Kong by Regent Publishing Services Limited
Printed in China by Leefung-Asco Printers Trading Limited

AUTHOR'S ACKNOWLEDGMENTS I would like to thank Sue Alexander, Roy Barrett, Reiko Castles, Lydie Roshem and Crystal Wells for their help with authenticating the recipes—and of course David, without whose support I couldn't achieve half of what I do.

Contents

Asian sauces and marinades

It is not surprising that Asia, home to around half the world's population, has produced some of the most diverse, exciting and inspirational cuisines in the world. When Asian people sit down to eat, they are not simply satisfying a craving for food. They are celebrating something even more fundamental to their culture and way of life—the ritual and pleasure of sharing food with family and friends.

At the heart of Asian cooking are the sauces and marinades that are integral to so many of its dishes. Pungent and richly spiced, aromatic with fresh herbs and fruit, sour with tamarind, or fired with the intense heat of chiles, every sauce is a complex and subtle masterpiece in its own right. Add to that the age-old custom of mothers handing down carefully guarded recipes to their daughters, never writing anything down or sharing their culinary secrets beyond the family, and the seemingly inscrutable puzzle that is Oriental cooking begins to deepen.

The aim of this book is to show that it is possible to unlock the secrets of Asian cuisines and that by a careful blend of ingredients and an understanding of the techniques that are used in Oriental cooking, you can create authentic Asian dishes in your own kitchen. Most of the ingredients called for in the recipes can be bought in supermarkets; more unusual ones can be tracked down in specialty stores or markets, or brought home as exciting culinary souvenirs from holidays to the East.

Although similar ingredients feature in cuisines all over Asia, different countries favor their own individual variations, either in the texture of soy sauce, the "heat" of curry paste, the saltiness of shrimp paste, or the pungency of fish sauce. It is these delicate differences and the manner in which ingredients are combined that make each individual Oriental cuisine unique.

External influences have also left their mark on the melting pot of Asia's cultures, its peoples, and, by extension, its cooking. Baguettes on sale in a Vietnamese market are a reminder of French colonial rule in Indochina. The Dutch introduced Indonesians to desserts and cakes, the Spanish added olive oil, tomatoes, olives and paella to Filipino kitchens, and Nyonya cuisine developed when the Chinese traders in Melaka and Singapore settled there and married Malay wives.

One of the defining flavors of Asian cooking is chile. This fruit of the capsicum plant grows prolifically all over the region and its liberal use, particularly in Thai, Indonesian, and Korean dishes, can make some recipes too hot for Western palates unaccustomed to such heat. There are hundreds of chile varieties and, as a general rule, heat can be measured in reverse proportion to size: the smaller the chile, the hotter it will be. This book approaches the quantity of chiles to be used in recipes with caution but, as with good wine, individual taste will dictate. If a recipe sounds too hot, cut the chiles down to suit your palate. You can always increase the amount next time, since you may well be surprised at how addictive chiles can become!

Asian cookery writers often compare the merits of a good meal with those of a good novel in that it must start well, have character and suspense, and follow through to a memorable finish. If this book can tempt you to discover more of the wonderful secrets of Asian cooking, a whole continent of evocative flavors and aromas is here to be explored and enjoyed in your own home.

As they say in China, chin, chin-ch'e. Bon appétit!

Glossary

Most of the special ingredients used in Asian cookery are available from larger supermarkets, specialty shops, and Oriental grocery stores.

ANNATTO The tiny red seeds of the "lipstick plant," used to color and flavor Asian dishes. The seeds are fried in oil to extract their orange color and the strained oil is used to dye foods.

BAMBOO SHOOTS More than 150 varieties of bamboo grass grow in China with the best-flavored shoots reputed to come from the eastern province of Zhejiang. The smallest, most flavorful shoots are dug just before they appear out of the ground in winter. Spring shoots resemble large asparagus spears, while bigger summer shoots are tougher and have less flavor. Usually sold canned in the West, they should be drained and rinsed before being added to recipes.

BEAN CURD See Fermented Bean Curd and Tofu.

BEAN SPROUTS The crisp sprouts grown from tiny green mung beans. They have a crunchy texture and a fresh, subtle taste. Sold fresh in plastic bags, they should be stored in the salad drawer of the refrigerator and used within 2 to 3 days. Once the shoots begin to turn brown they are no longer fresh and should be discarded. Used in stir-fries, noodle dishes, and soups, they only need brief cooking because, with their high water content, long cooking makes them soggy and tasteless.

BLACK BEANS Salted, fermented, soft black soy beans used in Chinese cooking particularly for black bean stir-fry sauce. Sold dry, in plastic bags or canned, they need to be rinsed or soaked to remove excess salt and chopped or crushed before use. Canned beans need to be drained from their canning liquid.

BONITO FLAKES Bonito fish (a member of the mackerel family) which is filleted and then dried until hard as wood before being shaved into fine flakes with a plane. The shaved flakes are sold as hana-katsuo in Japanese stores and are an essential ingredient in the soup stock, dashi.

CANDLENUTS Cream-colored and waxy, candlenuts are known as buah keras in Malaysia and kemiri in Indonesia, where they are ground and added to curry sauces in order to thicken them. If unavailable, macadamias, Brazil nuts, blanched almonds or cashews can be substituted.

CHILES Originally from the Americas, chiles traveled via Africa and India to the Far East. Red chiles are ripened green chiles and although they have a slightly different flavor, they can be equally fiery. A rich source of iron and vitamins A and C, chiles vary enormously in both size and heat but, as a general rule, the smaller the chile the hotter it will be. When preparing chiles take care to protect your hands either with thin rubber gloves or by washing them thoroughly immediately afterward and never touch your face or eyes because they can give nasty, stinging burns. Chiles can be bought fresh or dried and as a paste, powder, or sauce.

CHINESE CABBAGE Three types are most commonly used: white cabbage (bai cai, or bok choy in Cantonese), celery cabbage, which has long green feathery leaves and celery-like stems, and round cabbage.

CHINESE RICE WINE Archeological evidence suggests the Chinese have been making wine for more than four thousand years. Rice wine is made by fermenting rice, and ranges from mild and fragrant to powerful and sherry-like. Similar to dry sherry in its alcoholic content, it is only used in cooking or drunk in small quantities always with food. The wine from Shao Xing, a district south of Hangzhou, is generally considered to be the best. Dry sherry can be substituted in recipes. See also Mirin.

CHINESE 5-SPICE POWDER Used in Chinese dishes, it is a variable mix of five, and sometimes more, spices which are reputed to balance the ying and yang elements in dishes. Always included are star anise, fennel seeds, Szechwan peppercorns, cloves, and cinnamon or cassia

SAUCES AND PASTES 1 SHRIMP PASTE 2 OYSTER SAUCE 3 HOISIN SAUCE 4 SAMBAL OELEK 5 FISH SAUCE 6 TERIYAKI SAUCE 7 PLUM SAUCE 8 SOY SAUCE 9 WASABI PASTE

VEGETABLES AND FRUITS   **1** COCONUT   **2** CHINESE CABBAGE
3 SUGAR CANE   **4** LOTUS ROOT   **5** DAIKON   **6** BAMBOO SHOOTS (WHOLE, PEELED)   **7** CHILES
8 WATER CHESTNUTS   **9** BEANSPROUTS   **10** STRAW MUSHROOMS (CANNED)

bark, with coriander, ginger, and cardamom occasionally added as well.

CHIVES Chinese, coarse, or garlic chives all have much longer and flatter dark green leaves than the fine tubular chives we are more familiar with in the West. Garlic chives are sometimes available with their small white flowerheads still attached. Stronger than Western chives, they are best snipped with scissors or sliced with a very sharp cleaver, because chopping will bruise them.

CILANTRO The leaves are widely used in all Asian countries, and the Thais use the whole plant—leaves, seeds and roots. The roots are pounded with garlic and black pepper to make a basic seasoning in Thai dishes. Also known as coriander.

COCONUT Widely used in cooking in Thailand, Vietnam, Indonesia, and the Malay Peninsula. Grated coconut flesh is added to both sweet and savory recipes, as are coconut milk and cream. Asian recipe books will often specify "young coconut juice." This is not the sweet water inside a fresh coconut but is made by blending newly ripened coconut flesh and hot water and then straining the mixture through a fine sieve. Commercially prepared coconut milk is available in cans or dried in packs. Thicker "creamed" coconut is available as liquid in cartons or in block form, which needs to be dissolved in a little water before use.

DAIKON A large white radish frequently used raw in Japanese dishes. It is also pickled in rice bran and salt and added to sushi rolls or as part of a side dish of mixed pickles designed to cleanse the palate between richer foods. Also known as mooli.

DASHI A stock made from dried kelp and dried bonito flakes. The basis of Japanese soups and sauces. Can be bought as instant granules in jars and packages from Japanese stores, labelled dashi-no-moto.

DAUN KESUM A pungent Vietnamese herb with long, pointed green leaves tinged with purple. Used mainly in salads and other vegetable dishes.

DRIED SHRIMP Sun-dried, with a strong flavor and aroma. Used to season and flavor dishes. Dried shrimp should be soaked in warm water for an least an hour before use.

FERMENTED BEAN CURD Available in red and white styles. The red curd has ground red rice added to it, with the color on the surface only. Used to flavor and season marinades in dishes such as red-cooked Chinese roast pork.

FISH SAUCE A distinctive ingredient in Thai, Vietnamese and Filipino cooking made from salted, fermented fish or shrimp and rich in protein and B vitamins. Used in marinades, dressings, and dipping sauces, the best-quality ones are a rich golden brown in color and have a salty, pungent flavor. Known as nam pla in Thailand, nuoc mam in Vietnam, and patis in the Philippines. In these countries, fish sauce is often used in much the same way as soy sauce is used in China.

GALANGAL A member of the ginger family, used in Thai, Malay and Nyonya dishes. The tough skin needs to be peeled away before grinding or slicing. Young, pinkish roots have the best flavor.

GINGERROOT Available fresh as a root that needs to be peeled and grated, as a purée in jars, or dried and ground to a powder. Pickled red or pink ginger is used in Japanese dishes, particularly sushi. Special fresh gingerroot graters, which are finer than equivalent Western graters, can be bought from Oriental stores.

HOI SIN SAUCE A dark, thick, sweet sauce made with soy beans, spices, and garlic. Also known as Chinese Barbecue Sauce, it is used for brushing over meat as a seasoning or glaze, as a dipping sauce or in stir-fries.

KAFFIR LIME (LIME LEAVES) Very different to the smooth-skinned lime we are more familiar with in the West, the kaffir tree produces fruit with a knobbly rough skin, thick pith, and a hot, spicy, citrus flavor. The grated zest is added to food, and the leaves are added whole to flavor curries, soups and rice dishes. If added as an ingredient to a salad or other dish, the leaves must be sliced into the finest possible wafer-thin slices to make them edible.

KELP Japanese seaweed, also known as konbu, is an essential ingredient in dashi stock. Thick and glossy black-green in color, fresh kelp should only be wiped with paper towels before use so the surface flavor is not lost. Kelp should be removed just before a liquid comes to a boil to prevent it from imparting a bitter taste.

LAOS Another member of the ginger family made from a variety of galangal. Mild in flavor, it can be bought as a root or ground as a powder.

LEMONGRASS A lemon-scented plant that grows in clumps. Only the bottom 2 to 4 inches are used. If the stems are to be ground into a paste, the coarse outer leaves should be discarded first. If they are being added whole to a soup or stew, bruise the stems with a knife to release their flavor. Available in fresh, powdered, and puréed form, about one teaspoon of ready-prepared lemongrass equals one stalk. To make your own lemongrass purée, chop the lemongrass quite finely and process in a spice grinder with a little peanut oil.

LIME Limes grow plentifully in Southeast Asia and their rind and juice are used in countless ways. Many varieties are much smaller than the limes we are familiar with in the West. The kalamansi are generally considered to have the finest-flavored juice.

LOTUS The root of the Chinese lotus or water lily, which grows in lakes and ponds. The seeds and roots are harvested from late summer through fall and both are prized for their health-giving properties. The root has a crunchy texture and decorative lace-like appearance when sliced, making it a popular garnish for Japanese and Chinese dishes. The seeds are eaten as a sweet snack or sold dried for grinding into a sweet paste as a filling for cakes and buns. The blossom is used in restaurants for egg fu-yung dishes.

MIRIN A sweet rice wine fermented from medium-grain rice, glutinous rice and distilled rice spirit, and then matured for two months to produce its sweet flavor. Used in Japanese cooking, particularly dipping sauces. If it is not available, substitute one teaspoon sugar for one tablespoon mirin in a recipe.

MISO A salty paste of fermented soy beans which is rich in protein and the main ingredient of Japanese soups. Many different types are available, the most common being red or brown miso, which is reddish-brown in color with a strong flavor, and white miso, which is actually golden-yellow in color. The white has a lighter flavor and is less salty than the red. Red bean paste is also used in Korean dishes, where it is known as dhwen-jang.

MUSHROOMS Hundreds of different mushrooms grow across Southeast Asia, from tiny pinhead Japanese enoki to more "meaty" varieties such as shiitake and straw mushrooms. Dried Chinese mushrooms such as cloud ear fungus or black mushrooms need to be soaked in warm water before cooking. The soaking water can be added as stock to the dish being cooked, but it is important to strain it first to get rid of the grit.

NOODLES Sold both fresh and dried, and made from wheat flour, rice flour or mung bean flour. The most popular are: fresh yellow "hokkien," spaghetti-like and made from flour and egg; dried wheat-flour noodles; fresh flat rice-flour noodles; and dried rice-flour vermicelli, also known as rice-stick noodles. Dried mung bean noodles are used in soups and often referred to as "glass," "jelly" or "transparent" noodles. In Japan, wheat noodles or udon come in various widths and can be flat or round. Somen are also made from wheat but are very fine and white. Soba are made from buckwheat and are sometimes flavored with green tea. Translucent, jelly-like shirataki noodles, made from a root vegetable similar to yam, are used in one-pot dishes such as soups and sukiyaki.

OYSTER SAUCE A thick sauce made from ground oysters, water, salt, cornstarch, and caramel. It is used to flavor stir-fries and is very popular in Chinese cooking. It is worth looking for brands that do not include monosodium glutamate. Refrigerate after opening.

PALM SUGAR A raw sugar usually made from cane sugar and coconut palm sap. Also known as jaggery, the sap is boiled down until it crystallizes and is usually sold as a solid ball which should crumble easily rather than be rock-hard. Dark muscovado sugar or soft brown sugar makes a good substitute.

PLUM SAUCE Sold in cans or jars, this piquant reddish-brown condiment is made from salted plums, chiles, vinegar and sugar. Like oyster sauce, it must be refrigerated after opening.

RAMBUTAN A large lychee-like fruit from Thailand with red-brown hairy spikes all over the outer skin and the same dark glossy stone as a lychee. Similar in taste to the lychee, it is less juicy but can replace lychees in a fruit salad. Native to the Malay archipelago.

HERBS **1** CILANTRO **2** CHIVES **3** DAUN KESUM **4** GALANGAL
5 KAFFIR LIME LEAVES **6** LEMON GRASS

DRIED AND FERMENTED GOODS 1 KELP 2 CLOUD EAR FUNGUS 3 FERMENTED BEAN CURD (RED)
4 BLACK BEANS 5 DRIED SHRIMP 6 FERMENTED BEAN CURD (WHITE)

RED BEANS Dried adzuki beans used in Chinese and Japanese desserts or cooked with sugar to make red bean paste, which is a popular filling for buns and pancakes.

RICE The staple carbohydrate in most parts of Asia, with each country favoring its own style of rice. Long-grain is the most commonly used in Indonesia, Thailand, Vietnam, China, the Philippines, and Malaysia, while the Japanese favour short-grain rice to give the sticky consistency needed for sushi. Glutinous rice is preferred in north Thailand.

RICE PAPER A thin, translucent wrapper used to make Vietnamese spring rolls. It needs to be dampened to become soft and pliable enough to roll around a filling.

RICE VINEGAR Used extensively in Japanese and Chinese cooking. Chinese fermented rice vinegar is dark brown, Japanese is clear, light and sweet. Distilled grain vinegar, which is clear and stronger than rice vinegar, is also used in China. Drinking rice vinegar mixed with water has been a traditional Japanese hangover cure for centuries.

RICE WINE See Chinese Rice Wine, Mirin, Sake.

SAKE Japanese rice wine that is available in many different qualities. It is served from a bucket filled with warm water rather than ice cubes. Also added to cooked dishes, but the alcohol is always burned or heated off.

SAMBAL OELEK A fearsomely hot sauce used to fire up Indonesian dishes or serve as a relish. Made from red chiles minced with their seeds and mixed with vinegar and oil.

SESAME Available as oil, paste and seeds. The oil used in Chinese cooking is extracted from toasted seeds and pungently flavored so only a little is needed. It is usually drizzled over stir-fried dishes to add flavor rather than being used to cook the ingredients. Sesame seeds are a popular ingredient in Japanese, Chinese, and Korean cuisines. Black and white seeds are available.

SHRIMP PASTE Also known as kapi, trassi, trassie, terasi, ngapi, blacan and belacan, this dense mixture of fermented ground shrimp is used extensively in Southeast Asian cuisine. There are many different types ranging from pink to blackish-brown in color, the former being used for curries and the latter for dipping sauces. Shrimp paste should be cooked before eating.

SOY SAUCE The history of this ubiquitous Asian sauce can be traced back two thousand years. Used widely in all Far Eastern cuisines, styles vary from country to country. A good all-purpose brand is a Japanese naturally brewed soy sauce (shoyu) which is medium in strength, will not overwhelm other ingredients, and is neither too thick, too salty nor too sweet. Japanese cooks also use tamari, a strong, thick, black sauce with a distinctive, unique flavor. Lighter styles of soy sauce are popular in Thailand and Vietnam where dishes are more delicately flavored. In Indonesia kecap manis is thick, black, and syrupy ("manis" means sweet), while kecap asin is thinner and saltier. In China three types are used in cooking: light and dark are the most common, with a red soy sauce occasionally being added to give dishes a subtle flavor. Some cheaper brands of soy sauce have recently attracted unfavorable publicity due to their high levels of the chemical contaminant 3-MCPD, believed to cause cancer in rats, so it is advisable to seek out the better-known brands.

STAR ANISE A flower-shaped, dark brown seed pod with an aniseed flavor from a tree of the magnolia family. It grows mainly in southern China and is one of the most important everyday spices in Chinese cuisine. Used whole or broken into small pieces, it is added to marinades and sauces and discarded after cooking. It is also ground and added to Chinese 5-spice powder. Star anise is also said to relieve stomach pains, bladder problems and constipation.

STRAW MUSHROOMS Native to China, where they are widely cultivated in the south. Small with oval caps, they are available in cans from Oriental stores.

SUGAR CANE The tough outer bark of the canes is stripped away and the syrupy core is used for kebob skewers in Vietnamese dishes. As the "skewer" heats up, the syrup seeps out and flavors the food.

SZECHWAN PEPPER A round, reddish-brown berry with a distinctive fragrance and flavor. Used mainly in Chinese Szechwan cuisine and as an ingredient in Chinese 5-spice powder. It is often sold ground under its Japanese name, sansho.

TAMARIND The bean-shaped fruit of the tamarind tree. Available in sticky, dark brown blocks as a pulp that needs to be mixed with boiling water and strained before use. Also available as a concentrated paste in small spice jars. Tamarind adds a sour, mildly acidic flavor to dishes, similar to the sour taste of Worcestershire sauce, of which it is an important ingredient. It is widely used in Malaysian cuisine, particularly curries, where it is known as "asam."

TERIYAKI Japanese soy sauce flavored with rice wine and sugar. Used as a marinade or glaze for fish and meat dishes to be barbecued or roasted.

THAI BASIL Also known as "holy basil" or horapha, it is an Asian variety of the sweet basil that grows around the Mediterranean. It has a distinctive flavor of mild basil and aniseed, and has small, deep green oval shaped leaves with purple stems and flowers.

TOFU The Japanese name for bean curd. It is produced from the milky liquid from crushed soy beans which is then coagulated and pressed in a process similar to making cheese. Available in blocks as soft, firm, and smoked tofu. Silken tofu has a slightly more acidic flavor and a slightly firmer texture than soft tofu.

WASABI Green Japanese horseradish, available as a powder or paste. Very hot, the paste is usually sold in a tube from which it is squeezed onto serving plates in a small, decorative mound as a condiment to accompany sashimi and sushi.

WATER CHESTNUTS Dark-skinned, these chestnut-sized vegetables grow in water as their name suggests. Usually sold canned, they are white with a crisp texture and are a common ingredient in Asian cooking. Slice, julienne, or chop before adding to salads and stir-fries.

DRY GOODS **1** RICE-FLOUR NOODLES **2** RICE FLOUR VERMICELLI **3** PALM SUGAR **4** CHINESE 5-SPICE **5** STAR ANISE **6** SOBA NOODLES **7** RICE PAPER **8** ADZUKI BEANS **9** SZECHWAN PEPPER **10** WHEAT FLOUR NOODLES **11** WHOLEWHEAT FLOUR NOODLES

1 Marinades

A popular method of flavoring fish, poultry, meat, or bean curd (tofu). Marinades help tenderize meat through the addition of a natural acid such as wine, lemon juice or vinegar to the marinade mix. Contrasting sweet, sour, spicy, and salty ingredients are blended together, spooned over the food to be marinated, then left for several hours to enable the marinade ingredients to infuse and impart their flavors. Marinating is particularly useful when cooking with bean curd (tofu). Bland and without any distinctive flavor of its own, tofu absorbs other flavors easily. Marinating transforms it into a flavorful addition to stir-fries, braised or broiled dishes and curries.

Hoi sin, oyster sauce, and red bean curd marinade

Fermented red bean curd is added to sauces in Chinese cuisine but is very much an acquired taste for Western palates. The bean curd has ground red rice added to it and a flavor of strong cheese but the latter is well disguised when added to marinades as a seasoning. It is very salty, so only a little should be added to a dish.

Char siu is served as an appetizer rather than as a main course, with a dipping sauce such as plum or hoi sin. The pork can also be chopped into small pieces and added to dishes such as stir-fried rice, char siu buns, or spring rolls.

Mix all the ingredients together until evenly blended.

1 tbsp (15 mL) soft brown sugar
2 cloves garlic, peeled and minced
½ tsp (2 mL) finely grated gingerroot
2 tbsp (25 mL) hoi sin sauce
1 tbsp (15 mL) oyster sauce
½ tsp (2 mL) Chinese 5-spice powder
1 tbsp (15 mL) fermented red bean curd
2 tbsp (25 mL) rice wine or dry sherry

Char siu HONEY-ROAST RED-COOKED PORK

1 Trim all fat or sinew from the pork and cut into 1-in (2.5-cm) strips down the length of the meat. Place the strips side by side in a shallow dish and pour the marinade over them, turning the pork so it is well coated.
2 Cover and leave in a cool place for 2 to 3 hours, turning the strips over occasionally.
3 Preheat the oven to 425°F (220°C). Lift the pork from the dish (reserving the marinade) and put on a rack over a roasting pan. Pour in enough hot water to half-fill the pan and place in the oven for 15 minutes.
4 Reduce the oven temperature to 375°F (190°C). Brush the pork with the reserved marinade, turn the strips over and brush again, then drizzle with the melted honey. Cook for a further 15 minutes or until the pork is done and the honey has caramelized the outside to a light golden brown.
5 Cut into slices across the grain of the meat and serve with a dipping sauce, accompanied with shredded lettuce, cucumber slices, shredded scallions, and radishes. **SERVES 4 TO 6**

1 lb (450 g) pork fillet
1 quantity Hoi Sin, Oyster Sauce, and
   Red Bean Curd Marinade
2 tbsp (25 mL) clear honey, melted

SERVE WITH

Shredded iceberg lettuce
Cucumber slices
Shredded scallions and radishes

VARIATIONS Although the marinade is traditionally used to make char siu pork, it can also be used for glazing chicken kebobs, pork spareribs or other meat.

Ginger wine, soy, and coriander marinade

A Chinese-style marinade used to flavor fish or shellfish before stir-frying or steaming. Ginger is an indispensable part of Chinese cooking, believed to aid digestion, counteract the unwelcome symptoms of flatulence and prevent nausea.

When shelling the shrimp, leave on the tails. Devein by slitting down the back of each shrimp with a sharp knife and pulling out the dark thread-like "vein" running down the back. Cut almost all the way through the shrimps without cutting them quite in half, so they absorb as much of the marinade as possible and open out as they cook.

4 tbsp (50 mL) ginger wine
2 tbsp (25 mL) light soy sauce
1 tsp (5 mL) ground coriander

Mix the ingredients together.

Crystal shrimp

20 large raw shrimp, peeled and
    deveined, tails left on
1 quantity Ginger Wine, Soy, and
    Coriander Marinade
2 tbsp (25 mL) peanut oil
1 carrot, cut into thin strips
8 scallions, sliced

1 Place the shrimp in a shallow dish and pour the marinade over them. Cover and set aside in a cool place for 1 hour.
2 Heat the oil in a wok, add the carrot strips, and stir-fry for 2 to 3 minutes. Add the scallions and stir-fry for a further 2 minutes.
3 Add the shrimp, leaving any excess marinade in the dish. Stir-fry over brisk heat until the shrimp turn pink and curl. Pour in any remaining marinade and toss to coat the shrimp.
4 Serve immediately with boiled or stir-fried rice. SERVES 4

VARIATION Other shellfish such as scallops or baby squid can be used.

Palm sugar, garlic, and nuoc mam marinade

A typically Vietnamese mix of ingredients, used to marinate lean pork before braising it slowly in coconut milk in a wok. If palm sugar is not available, substitute with soft brown sugar.

The dish that goes with this marinade is a popular family meal, especially in France where there is a sizeable Vietnamese community who often refer to it as "porc au caramel." Use canned or reconstituted packaged coconut milk rather than the thicker coconut cream sold in cartons. Serve with steamed rice and a green vegetable.

Mix the ingredients together in a bowl until the sugar dissolves.

4 cloves garlic, peeled and minced
1 tbsp (15 mL) palm sugar or soft
  brown sugar
2 tbsp (25 mL) nuoc mam (Vietnamese
  fish sauce)

Thit heo kho nuoc dua

PORK AND EGG RAGOUT IN COCONUT MILK

1 Put the pork in a dish and add the marinade, turning the pieces of meat until coated. Set aside to marinate for 1 hour.
2 Heat the oil in a wok and briefly sear the pork in batches until lightly browned. Return all the batches of pork to the wok, add the soy sauce, the remaining marinade and the coconut milk. Stew gently for 45 minutes.
3 Add the eggs and cook for a further 15 minutes. **SERVES 4**

VARIATION Chicken can be cooked in the same way, but use legs or thighs rather than breasts, which would cook too quickly and become dry.

1½ lb (675 g) lean pork, cut into 2-in
  (5-cm) pieces
1 quantity Palm Sugar, Garlic, and
  Nuoc Mam Marinade
2 tbsp (25 mL) vegetable oil
2 tbsp (25 mL) soy sauce
4 cups (900 mL) coconut milk
4 hard-boiled eggs, shelled

Red pepper paste

6 tbsp (75 mL) dhwen-jang (Korean
red bean paste) or aka miso (Japanese
red bean paste)

2 tbsp (25 mL) sweet paprika

1 tsp (5 mL) chili powder (Korean,
if possible)

1½ tbsp (22 mL) soft brown sugar

Gochujang is half-relish, half-spice, and is an essential flavoring in Korean cooking. In the past, virtually every home would have had a large stone jar of the paste in the kitchen but, as with many things in the modern world, convenience has triumphed over tradition. Cooks now usually forgo the lengthy process of cooking glutinous rice powder with malt and blending it with fermented chili powder, ground soy beans and salt, in favor of buying ready-made paste in jars. This recipe is a simplified version of traditional gochujang paste.

When preparing the squid for this recipe, slit the body of each, open them out flat, and cut into even-sized squares or rectangles. Score the pieces on both sides in a criss-cross pattern with a sharp knife so they cook quickly and evenly and curl up in the pan with an attractive diamond pattern running round them.

Mix the ingredients together. Store in a sealed container in a cool place. The paste will keep for up to 6 months.

Oyi ngu bokum STIR-FRIED SEAFOOD WITH BELL PEPPERS

1 lb (450 g) cleaned squid, cut into
pieces and scored, tentacles sliced

4 tbsp (50 mL) peanut oil

1 red onion, peeled and thinly sliced

2 cloves garlic, peeled and chopped

1 red bell pepper, seeded and sliced

1 orange bell pepper, seeded and sliced

1 zucchini, chopped

1 tbsp (15 mL) Red Pepper Paste

6 scallops, halved

1 tsp (5 mL) sugar

1 tsp (5 mL) sesame oil

GARNISH WITH

1 tbsp (15 mL) chopped fresh cilantro

1 Bring a saucepan of water to a boil, add the squid, including sliced tentacles, and remove from the heat. Stir until the squid turns white then drain well.

2 Heat half the oil in a wok, add the onion and stir-fry for 3 to 4 minutes until it starts to soften. Add the garlic, bell peppers, and zucchini and stir-fry for 5 minutes. Remove from the pan and set aside.

3 Add the rest of the oil to the pan and stir in the Red Pepper Paste. Cook for 1 minute, then stir in the squid, scallops and sugar. Stir-fry for 2 to 3 minutes, then return the vegetables to the pan and toss together over the heat for 1 to 2 minutes. Sprinkle with the fresh cilantro and serve at once. SERVES 4

VARIATIONS Add other vegetables such as green beans or eggplant to the stir-fry instead of bell peppers and zucchini.

Sesame, soy, and ginger marinade

2 tbsp (25 mL) sesame seeds
½ tsp (2 mL) sea salt
6 scallions
1-in (2.5-cm) piece gingerroot,
    peeled and grated
2 cloves garlic, peeled and minced
4 tbsp (50 mL) Japanese soy sauce
2 tsp (10 mL) sesame oil
2 tsp (10 mL) soft brown sugar

Sesame seeds are used in so many Korean recipes that many cooks buy them in big tubs in the fall immediately after the harvest, when they are fresh, plentiful and cheap. Soy sauce is an essential flavoring in Korean dishes and while locally it comes in light, medium and dark varieties, in a Western kitchen shoyu (Japanese soy sauce) makes a good all-purpose alternative.

Use chicken thighs for this dish: they have a better texture and flavor than other cuts when used in a slow-cooked dish such as a braise or stew. Skin the thighs or not, as you prefer.

1 Heat a small, heavy skillet over low heat. Add the sesame seeds and stir until they begin to turn golden and give off a toasted, nutty aroma. Transfer to a mortar and pestle and crush with the salt.
2 Trim the scallions and cut off the green tops, reserving these to garnish the finished dish. Chop the white parts very finely.
3 Mix the crushed sesame seeds with the chopped scallions, ginger, garlic, soy sauce, sesame oil and sugar.

Takpokkum SOY AND SESAME BRAISED CHICKEN

8 chicken thighs
1 quantity Sesame, Soy, and
    Ginger Marinade
2 tbsp (25 mL) vegetable oil
About 2 cups (450 mL) chicken stock
1 red bell pepper, seeded and chopped

GARNISH WITH

Green parts of scallions reserved from
    sauce recipe above

1 Cut several slashes in each chicken thigh and place them side by side in a shallow dish. Pour the marinade over the chicken and turn until coated. Cover and leave in a cool place for 4 to 5 hours, turning from time to time.
2 Heat the oil in a large deep skillet with a lid. Lift the chicken from the marinade dish and brown on both sides in the pan. Pour in remaining marinade and add enough stock to just cover the chicken.
3 Cover and cook gently for 20 minutes. Add the bell pepper and simmer uncovered for a further 15 minutes until the chicken is very tender and the sauce has reduced.
4 Slice the scallion tops thinly on the diagonal and sprinkle over the chicken. Serve with a green leafy vegetable. **SERVES 4**

VARIATION Add other vegetables such as thinly sliced carrots, chopped zucchini, or baby corn to the dish, adjusting the cooking time as necessary.

2 Stir-fry sauces

Stir-frying is an important cooking technique used all over Southeast Asia. Unlike many Western dishes that require last minute carving or portioning when brought to the table, Asian food is generally served ready to eat, as all the chopping, slicing and shredding take place during the preparation. The round base of a wok makes it the ideal pan for stir-frying because ingredients can be tossed rapidly over the heat without fear of splashes or spills. Meat, vegetables, fish or seafood are first cut into even-sized pieces so that when they are added to the hot wok they cook quickly and evenly without losing their flavor, texture and nutrients. Once the stir-fry is cooked, a sweet or sour sauce is poured into the wok (sometimes the mixture that has been used to marinate the ingredients first), then everything is mixed together quickly and the dish is served immediately.

Garlic, fresh cilantro, and chile sauce

½-oz (15-g) bunch fresh cilantro

4 cloves garlic, peeled and minced

1 medium red chile, seeded and
    finely chopped

¼ cup (100 mL) vegetable oil

This sauce is made with three ingredients that are ubiquitous in Thai cuisine. Add extra chiles if you like things hot!

Pad thai is probably Thailand's most famous noodle dish. Like most Oriental recipes, its spelling will vary according to the part of the country you are in and who your translator is. Choose medium-sized shrimp rather than the very large ones. The peanuts should be natural, unsalted, and roasted in a dry, heavy skillet until golden. Take care not to burn them or they will have a bitter taste.

Remove the leaves from the fresh cilantro and chop coarsely. Chop the stalks finely. Mix with the chile and vegetable oil.

Pad thai

12 oz (350 g) medium flat rice noodles

1 quantity Garlic, Fresh Cilantro,
    and Chile Sauce

9 oz (250 g) raw shrimp, peeled and
    coarsely chopped

4 shallots, peeled and sliced

1 tbsp (15 mL) sugar

4 large eggs, beaten

1 tbsp (15 mL) oyster sauce

2 tbsp (25 mL) nam pla (Thai fish sauce)

Juice of 1 lime

9 oz (250 g) bean sprouts

4 scallions, shredded

1 cup (250 mL) unsalted, roasted
    peanuts, roughly chopped

1 Cook or soak the rice noodles according to the package instructions, then drain and set aside.

2 Heat the sauce in a pan. When hot, add the shrimp and shallots and stir-fry for 1 minute. Add the sugar and eggs and cook for a further 1 minute, stirring frequently.

3 Add the oyster sauce, fish sauce, lime juice, and drained noodles. Stir-fry for 2 minutes. Add the bean sprouts, scallions, and half the peanuts, and toss everything together over the heat until piping hot.

4 Spoon onto serving plates, sprinkle with the rest of the peanuts, and serve at once. **SERVES 4**

VARIATIONS Replace the shrimp with shredded chicken. For a vegetarian dish, add extra vegetables such as carrots, shredded bok choy, or snow peas.

Sweet and sour stir-fry sauce

½ cup (100 mL) chicken stock

3 tbsp (45 mL) rice vinegar

1 tbsp (15 mL) clear honey

1 tbsp (15 mL) dark soy sauce

2 tbsp (25 mL) light soy sauce

2 tbsp (25 mL) tomato sauce or ketchup

1 tsp (5 mL) cornstarch

Probably the most famous—and abused—Chinese meal in the West is Sweet and Sour Pork. Often made with fatty meat, lumpy batter, and a fluorescent sauce, it bears little resemblance to the original sweet and sour sauce, which should be glistening and translucent with a tangy flavor. The sauce also works well with chicken, spareribs, shrimp or mixed stir-fried vegetables.

Medium-sized or jumbo shrimp are both suitable for this recipe but it is important to stir-fry them briskly over high heat so they seal quickly and do not overcook. After stir-frying, the shrimp and vegetables are braised briefly in the sauce so they absorb all its flavors. Serve with plain steamed or boiled rice.

Place all the ingredients except the cornstarch in a saucepan and heat gently. Mix the cornstarch with 1 tablespoon of water, add to the pan, and stir continuously until the sauce bubbles and thickens. Simmer for 1 minute, then remove from the heat.

Gwoo lo har CANTONESE SWEET AND SOUR SHRIMP

2 tbsp (25 mL) peanut oil

5 tbsp (65 mL) raw cashew nuts

1 garlic clove, peeled and finely chopped

1-in (2.5-cm) piece gingerroot, peeled and grated

1 red bell pepper, seeded and chopped

6 oz (175 g) canned water chestnuts, rinsed and chopped

8 scallions, trimmed and cut into 1-in (2.5-cm) lengths

1 lb (450 g) raw shrimp, peeled and deveined

1 quantity Sweet and Sour Stir-Fry Sauce

1 Heat the oil in a wok, add the cashew nuts, and stir-fry for about 30 seconds until golden. Remove and drain on paper towels.

2 Add the garlic, ginger, bell pepper, and water chestnuts to the pan and stir-fry for 3 minutes. Add the scallions and stir-fry for 1 minute. Add the shrimp and stir-fry for a further 1 minute.

3 Pour in the sauce, toss the ingredients until coated, and simmer for 2 minutes. Sprinkle with cashews and serve immediately. **SERVES 4**

VARIATION If using pork, choose lean steaks and cut into thin strips or cubes. Stir-fry over brisk heat for 2 to 3 minutes to brown after you have removed the cashews from the wok, then remove and fry the vegetables. Return the pork to the wok with the sauce.

Garlic, fish sauce, and lime stir-fry sauce

Three flavors that are indigenous to Thai cuisine combine to form the basis of a hot, salty, sweet and sour sauce for stir-frying pork, chicken or mixed vegetables. As many Thais rely on taste rather than formal recipes, the quantity of chiles and other spices added will depend on the cook's personal preference, so add more or less seasoning as preferred.

The basis of Mee krob is vermicelli, sold dried in rolls and bound together in bundles. To separate the amount needed for a recipe, simply snip off the noodles with sharp kitchen scissors. The vermicelli need to be soaked briefly in cold water to soften them, but they must then be dried thoroughly before frying or they will spit dangerously when added to the hot oil. It is also important to heat the oil to the correct temperature or the vermicelli will be tough and chewy rather than crisp. If you don't have a cooking thermometer, place the handle of a wooden spoon in the hot oil; when bubbles form around it, the oil is ready.

Mix the ingredients together, stirring until the sugar dissolves.

Juice of 1 lime
1 tsp (5 mL) fresh garlic purée
1 tbsp (15 mL) soft brown sugar
2 red chiles, seeded and finely chopped
3 tbsp (45 mL) nam pla (Thai fish sauce)
1 tbsp (15 mL) rice vinegar

Mee krob CRISPY FRIED RICE VERMICELLI

1 Snip the vermicelli into short lengths and soak briefly in cold water to soften. Dry thoroughly on paper towels.
2 Heat oil for deep-frying in a wok to 375°F (190°C), add the vermicelli a little at a time, and fry until they are lightly golden and crisp. Drain on paper towels.
3 Pour off most of the oil from the wok, leaving about 2 tablespoons. Reheat, add the pork, and stir-fry for 2 minutes over brisk heat. Add the chicken and stir-fry for 3 minutes. Remove and set aside.
4 Add the red bell pepper and snow peas and stir-fry for 3 minutes. Return the pork and chicken to the wok and add the sauce. Toss for 1 minute, then add the eggs and stir until they have set.
5 Add the noodles and herbs and toss together over the heat until well mixed. Serve at once before the noodles have started to soften. **SERVES 4**

7 oz (200 g) rice vermicelli
Peanut oil for deep-frying
6 oz (175 g) lean pork, cut into small pieces
2 chicken breasts, skinned and cut into small pieces
1 red bell pepper, seeded and chopped
4 oz (100 g) snow peas, sliced
1 quantity Garlic, Fish Sauce, and Lime Stir-fry Sauce
2 large eggs, beaten
2 tbsp (25 mL) chopped fresh cilantro
1 tbsp (15 mL) snipped fresh chives

VARIATIONS As with most stir-fries, you may vary the ingredients according to their availability. Shrimp, diced firm tofu, ground turkey, and other vegetables such as finely sliced carrots, chopped baby corn and shredded scallions can also be used.

Plum sauce

Tangy and sweet at the same time, this reddish-brown stir-fry sauce is the perfect partner for rich meats like duck and goose. Although time-consuming to make, it stores well, and can be kept for several months in the refrigerator even after opening.

Two versions of this Cantonese duck dish are popular in China. One is made with a whole raw duck that is steamed, the other with ready-roasted duck meat. This recipe falls somewhere between the two because it uses raw duck breasts that are broiled and sliced prior to stir-frying.

2 lb (900 g) dark red plums, pitted and chopped

¾ cup (175 mL) raisins

8 oz (225 g) onions, peeled and chopped

2 medium red or green chiles, seeded and coarsely chopped

2 tsp (10 mL) fresh ginger purée

1 tsp (5 mL) allspice

1 tbsp (15 mL) black peppercorns, crushed

½ tsp (2 mL) ground cloves

2 pt (1.2 L) distilled malt vinegar

1 tbsp (15 mL) salt

4 cups (900 mL) demerara sugar

1 Put the plums in a preserving saucepan with the raisins, onions, chiles, ginger, allspice, crushed peppercorns, and cloves. Pour in the vinegar and bring to a boil. Lower the heat and simmer for 45 minutes.
2 Cool a little, then purée the contents of the pan and strain back into the pan. Add the salt and sugar and stir over the heat until the sugar dissolves.
3 Simmer for 2 hours or until thick with no excess liquid on the surface. Pour into warmed bottles and seal. **MAKES 3¾ CUPS (850 ML)**

Ba law lychee a CANTONESE DUCK WITH LYCHEES AND PINEAPPLE

2 duck breasts, skin on

1 tsp (5 mL) ground coriander

1 tsp (5 mL) Chinese 5-spice powder

2 tbsp (25 mL) peanut oil

1 red onion, peeled and sliced

1 carrot, peeled and cut into matchsticks

2 oz (50 g) snow peas

1 slice pineapple, cut into small pieces

8 lychees, peeled, pitted and halved

4 tbsp (50 mL) Plum Sauce

1 Dust the duck breasts with the ground coriander and Chinese 5-spice powder. Cook in a cast-iron grill pan or under a conventional broiler for about 10 minutes or until almost done, turning once or twice. Transfer to a board, allow to rest for 5 minutes, then slice the duck as thinly as possible.
2 Heat the oil in a wok, add the onion and stir-fry for 3 minutes. Add the carrot and stir-fry for 2 minutes, then add the snow peas and stir-fry for a further 2 minutes.
3 Add the duck, pineapple pieces, lychees, and Plum Sauce and stir-fry for 2 minutes. Serve at once with boiled rice. **SERVES 4**

VARIATION Although best suited to the richness of duck, Plum Sauce could also be used in stir-fried chicken, pork, or turkey dishes.

Black bean sauce

Chinese black beans are fermented, salted soy beans and can be found in cans in Oriental food stores. Dried beans are also available but must be soaked before use. Drain the canned beans and soak in cold water for 30 minutes before using.

As with most commercially prepared sauces, the black bean sauce you make yourself will taste fresher and be more aromatic than anything you find on a supermarket shelf. Serve this popular beef dish with rice noodles topped with finely chopped red chile and shredded scallions.

Soak the beans in cold water for 30 minutes. Drain and rinse. Purée with the other ingredients until smooth.

2 tbsp (25 mL) canned black beans

2 cloves garlic, peeled and chopped

1-in (2.5-cm) piece gingerroot,
  peeled and grated

1 red chile, seeded and chopped

1 tsp (5 mL) sesame oil

2 tbsp (25 mL) dark soy sauce

1 tsp (5 mL) sugar

1 tbsp (15 mL) rice wine or dry sherry

1 tbsp (15 mL) oyster sauce

¼ cup (50 mL) water

See jup ngau yook BEEF IN BLACK BEAN SAUCE

1 Wrap the beef tightly in plastic wrap and place in the freezer for 1 hour or until firm enough to cut into very thin strips across the grain of the meat. Heat the oil in a wok, add the beef, and stir-fry over high heat for 2 to 3 minutes.

2 Add the Black Bean Sauce, lower the heat, and cook for a further 2 minutes, stirring frequently.

3 Blend the water with the cornstarch until smooth and pour into the pan. Stir until the sauce thickens and clears. Serve at once with rice noodles.

SERVES 4

1 lb (450 g) sirloin or fillet steak,
  trimmed of any fat

2 tbsp (25 mL) peanut oil

1 quantity Black Bean Sauce

1 tbsp (15 mL) cold water

1 tsp (5 mL) cornstarch

VARIATIONS Although beef is by far the most popular meat for serving with black bean sauce, pork and chicken can also be used. The sauce also works well as a marinade for spareribs.

GRAVY

CHICKEN BROTH   L CUP
DK SOY   1 - 1½ T
LT SOY (SANG CHAU) 1 - 1½ T
OYSTER SAUCE   1 - 1½ T
CORNSTARCH -   2 - 3 +

Dark soy, ginger, and sesame sauce

As with most other Asian cuisines, soy sauce is an essential flavoring and seasoning ingredient in Korean dishes. Light, medium and dark versions are used, with the lighter ones usually the saltiest and thinnest. A naturally fermented medium Japanese soy sauce can be used in this recipe if Korean is not available.

Tak contains sesame oil which adds a wonderfully aromatic flavor but, as the strengths of different oils can vary, it is important to add a little at a time to prevent a strongly flavored oil from overwhelming the other ingredients.

Whisk the soy sauce, sugar, ginger, black pepper, and sesame seeds together until the sugar dissolves.

3 tbsp (45 mL) soy sauce

1 tbsp (15 mL) sugar

2 tsp (10 mL) fresh ginger purée

Black pepper to taste

1 tbsp (15 mL) sesame seeds

Tak STIR-FRIED CHICKEN WITH SHREDDED OMELET

3 boneless chicken breasts, skinned and cut into strips

1 quantity Dark Soy, Ginger, and Sesame Sauce

6 tbsp (90 mL) vegetable oil

1 carrot, cut into matchsticks

1 red bell pepper, seeded and sliced

7 oz (200 g) shiitake mushrooms, sliced

6 scallions, thinly sliced

1 tsp (5 mL) sesame oil

1 egg, lightly beaten

1 Place the chicken in a shallow dish, cover it with the sauce, and turn the chicken pieces until coated. Set aside for 1 hour.
2 Lift the chicken from the dish, reserving the marinade.
3 Heat half the vegetable oil in a wok, add the sliced carrot and red bell pepper, and stir-fry for 5 minutes. Add the mushrooms and scallions and stir-fry for a further 5 minutes. Remove vegetables from the wok and set aside.
4 Drizzle the sesame oil into the wok and, when the oil is hot, stir-fry the chicken for 2 to 3 minutes. Return the vegetables to the pan along with the marinade and bring to a boil. Simmer over low heat while you prepare the shredded omelet.
5 Heat the remaining vegetable oil in a large non-stick skillet and pour in the egg. Tilt the pan so the egg coats the base in a wafer-thin layer. Fry until set underneath, then flip over to set the other side. Slide out of the skillet onto a board and roll up. Slice as thinly as possible with a small serrated knife and sprinkle the omelet strips over the chicken and vegetables. Serve at once. **SERVES 4**

VARIATIONS Instead of the vegetables suggested, experiment with other combinations such as green beans, cauliflower, and cherry tomato halves or broccoli, bean sprouts, and yellow zucchini. If using cauliflower or broccoli, divide into tiny florets and blanch them first until just tender.

Tamarind sauce

Tamarind's astringency makes it a popular seasoning in many Vietnamese sauces. In this recipe for Tamarind sauce, it is combined with nuoc mam, the ingredient that defines the country's cuisine more than any other. Produced from the liquid drained from salted, fermented fish, it gives Vietnamese cooking a distinctive flavor. Like fine wine, the longer the liquor has been stored and aged the more highly it is prized.

Crab is the perfect accompaniment for this sauce and should be stir-fried in its shell so the delicate meat is protected from the hot oil. Buy freshly cooked crabs from your fish merchant (or crab claws, if available). Remove the tail flap, stomach sac, and feathery gray gills before cutting the crabs into large pieces with a heavy knife or cleaver.

Warm the rice wine and when it comes to simmering point, pour it over the tamarind pulp and leave to infuse for 15 minutes. Strain and mix in the fish sauce, lemongrass purée, garlic, and sugar.

⅔ cup (150 mL) rice wine or dry sherry

1 tbsp (15 mL) tamarind pulp

2 tbsp (25 mL) nuoc mam (Vietnamese fish sauce)

1 tsp (5 mL) fresh lemongrass purée

1 garlic clove, peeled and minced

1 tsp (5 mL) soft brown sugar

Cua rang voi sot me CRAB WITH TAMARIND SAUCE

1 Heat the oil in a wok, add the crab pieces, and stir-fry over brisk heat for 3 to 4 minutes. Add the scallions and tomatoes and cook for a further 2 minutes, stirring frequently.

2 Pour in the sauce and toss together so it coats the crab and vegetables. Cook for 2 minutes until the sauce bubbles and reduces a little. Transfer to a serving dish and serve with boiled rice and steamed or stir-fried vegetables.

SERVES 4

2 tbsp (25 mL) peanut oil

2 large freshly cooked crabs in the shell, cleaned and cut into large pieces

4 scallions, sliced

3 plum tomatoes, quartered

1 quantity Tamarind Sauce

VARIATION Shrimp can be substituted for the crab. Use about 1 lb (450 g) medium-sized shrimp, and peel if raw or leave in their shells if already cooked. Stir-fry raw shrimp for about 5 minutes until they turn pink and cooked shrimp for 2 to 3 minutes so they just heat through.

Sweet chile and tomato sauce

1 tbsp (15 mL) peanut oil

2 cloves garlic, peeled and minced

1 tsp (5 mL) grated fresh gingerroot

1 tsp (5 mL) sweet chile sauce

4 tbsp (50 mL) tomato sauce or ketchup

1 tbsp (15 mL) soy sauce

1 tbsp (15 mL) rice wine or dry sherry

Fast food for Singaporeans means a stop at a hawker stall where vendors will satisfy customers' hunger pangs by stir-frying, steaming, chopping, or barbecuing an array of freshly prepared ingredients to order. The large Chinese population means stir-fries are very popular, and this spicy blend of chile, garlic, and tomato is a typical sauce for stir-fries.

Kway teow are rice noodles, also known as rice sticks or ribbon noodles depending on whether they are round or flat. Cook them in boiling water for 3 to 4 minutes until tender and once they are ready, drain in a colander under running cold water and rub them gently between your fingers so they do not stick together. Leave the noodles in the colander until you are ready to add them to the wok.

Heat the oil in a pan and fry the garlic and ginger over low heat for 2 to 3 minutes. Add the remaining ingredients, stir well and bring to a boil. Simmer for 1 minute, then remove from the heat.

Char kway teow SINGAPORE FRIED RICE NOODLES

2 tbsp (25 mL) peanut oil

8 oz (225 g) pork steaks, cut
   into thin strips

1 green bell pepper, seeded and sliced

2 shallots, peeled and sliced

6 oz (175 g) bean sprouts

6 oz (175 g) shiitake mushrooms,
   quartered or sliced

8 oz (225 g) raw tiger shrimp, peeled and
   deveined

11 oz (300 g) flat rice noodles, cooked

1 quantity Sweet Chile and Tomato Sauce

GARNISH WITH

4 finely sliced or shredded scallions

1 Heat the oil in a wok, add the pork strips, and stir-fry over brisk heat for 4 to 5 minutes. Remove from the pan and set aside.
2 Add the bell pepper, shallots and bean sprouts and stir-fry for 3 minutes. Add the mushrooms and shrimp and stir-fry for a further 2 minutes until the vegetables are starting to soften and the shrimp turn pink.
3 Return the pork to the pan, add the noodles, and pour on the sauce. Toss together over the heat until everything is well combined and piping hot. Sprinkle with the scallions and serve at once. **SERVES 4**

VARIATION Beef with fried rice noodles makes another popular stall dish in Singapore.

3 Dressings and pickling sauces

With a wide variety of fresh vegetables and fruit readily available, it is not surprising that crisp, colorful salads are very popular in Southeast Asia. Vendors at Thai street food stalls prepare green papaya salad to order for workers needing a quick lunch; the Vietnamese might prefer the crunchy, celery-like stem of the lotus flower, a symbol of purity. Dressings are flavored with pungent fish sauce and hot chiles, which are then soothed by the sweetness of palm sugar and the cooling crunch of green leaves and vegetables. By contrast, in the cooler climes of Japan, Korea and north Vietnam, vegetables need to be pickled so they will last through the winter months. One of the most famous vegetable pickles is kimchi, a Korean brine-pickled cabbage that is almost the country's national dish and is served at every meal.

Chile peanut dressing

A variation on the peanut sauce that accompanies satay (see page 124), this spicy salad dressing is served spooned over an Indonesian mixed vegetable salad called Gado-gado.

Vegetables that cannot be eaten raw would usually be steamed to retain all their texture and flavor, but they could be blanched or boiled in a saucepan of water if preferred. The dish makes an excellent addition to a buffet table, especially if you are entertaining vegetarian guests.

1 Heat the oil in a skillet and stir-fry the peanuts until golden. Remove immediately from the pan with a slotted spoon, reserving 2 tablespoons of the oil. Drain the nuts on paper towels and allow to cool. Grind coarsely in a food processor or mortar and pestle.

2 Mix the lemongrass purée, garlic, shallots, chile and shrimp paste together.

3 Reheat the reserved oil, add the garlic and shallot mixture, and cook for 2 minutes, stirring frequently. Add the coconut milk, lime juice, sugar, soy sauce, ground peanuts, and water and cook over low heat for 10 minutes, stirring frequently.

4 tbsp (50 mL) peanut oil
1 cup (225 mL) unroasted, unsalted peanuts
1 tsp (5 mL) fresh lemongrass purée
2 cloves garlic, peeled and minced
2 shallots, peeled and finely chopped
1 medium red chile, seeded and finely chopped
¼ tsp (1 mL) shrimp paste
⅔ cup (150 mL) coconut milk
Juice of 1 lime
2 tsp (10 mL) soft brown sugar
2 tsp (10 mL) dark soy sauce
1¼ cups (300 mL) water

Gado-gado VEGETABLE SALAD WITH CHILE PEANUT DRESSING

1 Steam or boil the carrot and potato until tender. Drain and cool under cold water. Steam or blanch the green beans and bean sprouts for 1 minute. Drain and refresh under cold water.

2 Place the carrot, potato, beans, bean sprouts, mooli, and pineapple in a bowl and toss together.

3 Arrange the Chinese cabbage and white cabbage in a serving bowl and arrange the vegetables and pineapple in the center.

4 Dilute the dressing with extra warm water if necessary. Cool and spoon over the salad. Garnish with the hard-boiled eggs, cucumber, and fresh cilantro sprigs. Serve right away. **SERVES 4**

1 medium carrot, peeled and thinly sliced
1 large potato, peeled and diced
4 oz (100 g) green beans, cut into 1-in (2.5-cm) lengths
4 oz (100 g) bean sprouts, rinsed
5 oz (150 g) mooli (white radish), peeled and cut into matchsticks
1 slice pineapple, cut into small chunks
4 oz (100 g) Chinese cabbage, finely shredded
2 oz (50 g) white cabbage, finely shredded
1 quantity Chile Peanut Dressing

GARNISH WITH

2 hard-boiled eggs, quartered or sliced
4 oz (100 g) cucumber, sliced or chopped
Fresh cilantro sprigs

VARIATIONS Shredded spiced chicken could be added to the salad for a non-vegetarian dish. Fry two chicken breasts in a little oil, or cook in a ridged grill pan, sprinkling with 1 tablespoon ground coriander and ½ teaspoon chili powder. When done, cool the chicken, then cut into thin slices and arrange over the salad.

Chinese pickling brine

1 lb 2 oz (500 g) granulated sugar

2½ cups (600 mL) distilled white vinegar

1 tsp (5 mL) salt

1¼ cups (300 mL) water

1 tbsp (15 mL) Szechwan peppercorns

Food is preserved in many different ways in China. Fish, meat, eggs, vegetables, and fruit can all be dried, salted, smoked, or pickled to ensure they keep for another day. This brine is for pickling vegetables to be served as an accompaniment or garnish to other dishes.

For this vegetarian pickle, select fresh, unblemished vegetables and prepare by cutting them into even-sized pieces. Different vegetables can be used but the more contrasting colors you have, the more attractive the finished pickle.

Place all the ingredients in a saucepan and heat gently until the sugar has dissolved, stirring occasionally. Bring to a boil, then remove from the heat and allow to cool.

Suen soh choi MIXED PICKLED VEGETABLES

2½ lb (1.2 kg) mixed vegetables, e.g., carrots, daikon (white radish), red bell peppers, cucumber, celery, cauliflower, baby corn

2-in (5-cm) piece gingerroot, peeled and cut into fine matchsticks

1 quantity cold Chinese Pickling Brine

1 Prepare the vegetables as necessary; cut carrots, radish, and cucumber into matchsticks, bell peppers into small diamonds, celery into slices, cauliflower into small florets, and baby corn into small chunks. Rinse well.

2 Bring a large saucepan of water to a rolling boil, add the prepared vegetables, bring back to a boil, then remove from the heat straight away. Leave for 2 minutes, then drain.

3 Pat the vegetables with paper towels to remove excess water. Spread them out on more paper on a wire rack and allow to dry completely.

4 Pack the vegetables into preserving jars and pour the pickling brine over them to cover completely.

5 Store in the refrigerator for 1 week before using. SERVES 12

VARIATION Add a couple of slit whole chiles to the jars if you prefer a spicier pickle.

Korean pickling mix

Kimchi is a spicy vegetable relish considered a vital part of every Korean meal, even breakfast. Added to soups, casseroles, pancakes, and stir-fries, it is also served on its own as a side dish and there are scores of different versions. In the museum in Seoul there is a section devoted solely to kimchi, with 160 different varieties made from vegetables such as bok choy, white radish, cucumber and Chinese turnip. Cooks who prefer not to make their own can buy bottled kimchi.

When the Korean cabbage and red chile crops are harvested around late November entire villages set about making their supply of kimchi for the winter. Using a pickling process similar to that used for sauerkraut, cabbages and other vegetables are shredded and brined, often with salted shrimp and oysters between the vegetable layers, in huge vats where they seethe and ferment until sour. In the countryside, vats are buried to prevent the pickle from freezing when the temperature drops, and in cities they adorn balconies and terraces.

See below for method.

6¼ cups (1.5 L) water

Sea salt

6 scallions, trimmed and thinly sliced

4 cloves garlic, peeled and minced

2 tbsp (25 mL) grated gingerroot

1 tsp (5 mL) cayenne pepper

2 tsp (10 mL) paprika

1 tsp (5 mL) sugar

Kimchi PICKLED CHINESE CABBAGE AND DAIKON

1 Quarter the cabbage lengthwise, then cut each quarter across into roughly 2-in (5-cm) pieces. Peel the daikon, halve lengthwise, and slice into thin strips.
2 Put the water for the pickling mix in a large bowl and stir in 3 tablespoons salt until dissolved. Add the cabbage and daikon and weight down with a plate so they stay submerged. Cover and leave for 12 hours, stirring occasionally.
3 Using a slotted spoon, lift the cabbage and daikon from the bowl, reserving the salted water. Mix the vegetables with the remaining ingredients from the pickling mix, plus 1 teaspoon of salt. Pack into two 5-cup (1.1-L) jars or one larger jar.
4 Pour in enough of the reserved salted water to cover the vegetables, leaving a 1-in (2.5-cm) space at the top of the jars. Cover loosely with a non-metallic lid and leave in a cool place for 3 days or until the pickle has soured enough for your taste.
5 Cover tightly and keep in a cold, dark place for up to six months.
MAKES TWO 5-CUP (1.1-L) JARS

1½ lb (675 g) Chinese cabbage

8 oz (225 g) daikon (white radish)

1 quantity Korean Pickling Mix

VARIATION Other shredded vegetables such as cucumber and turnip can replace some of the cabbage.

8 oz (225 g) cooking apples, peeled,
   cored and chopped

4 shallots, peeled and sliced

2 cloves garlic, peeled and chopped

1-in (2.5-cm) piece gingerroot,
   peeled and grated

1 tsp (5 mL) salt

1 cup (225 mL) soft brown sugar

2¼ cups (500 mL) distilled white vinegar

1 to 2 papayas, total weight about 1 lb or
   2 oz (500 g), when seeded, peeled and
   chopped

2 cups (225 mL) besan (chickpea flour)
   or all-purpose whole-wheat flour

1 tsp (5 mL) salt

1 tsp (5 mL) garam masala

1 tsp (5 mL) ground coriander

1 tsp (5 mL) ground cumin

½ tsp (2 mL) chili powder

About 2 cups (450 mL) cold water

2 egg whites, beaten until standing in
   soft peaks

2 lb (900 g) mixed vegetables cut into
   bite-sized pieces, e.g., cauliflower
   florets, eggplants, zucchini, potatoes,
   baby carrots

Vegetable oil for deep-frying

SERVE WITH

Papaya Chutney

Papaya chutney

It is best to use underripe papayas for this relish or the finished chutney will be too sweet. To prepare papayas, cut in half, scoop out the shiny black seeds and membrane in the center, and peel away the outer green skin.

The planting of rubber trees across the Malay Peninsula brought an influx of laborers from India and Sri Lanka who came to work on the plantations as tappers, bringing with them not just their beliefs and lifestyles but their culinary heritage as well. These crisp vegetable fritters, or pakoras, would be served as a snack in Malaysia but they would make a good appetizer or side dish for a curry meal.

Put the apples, shallots, garlic, ginger, salt, sugar, and vinegar in a saucepan and simmer until the apples and shallots are soft. Add the papaya and continue to simmer until the chutney is thick, with no excess liquid on the surface. Stir well and bottle in clean, sterilized jars.

MAKES ABOUT 1½ LB (675 G)

Pakoras with papaya chutney

1 Sift the flour, salt and spices into a bowl and gradually mix in the water with a wooden spoon to make a smooth batter the consistency of unwhipped heavy cream. Fold in the beaten egg whites.
Blanch firmer vegetables such as cauliflower florets, potato pieces, and baby carrots in a saucepan of boiling water for 5 minutes; softer vegetables such as eggplants and zucchini can be dipped in the batter without blanching.
2 Heat vegetable oil for deep-frying to 375°F (190°C). Dip the vegetables in the batter, one piece at a time, and place in the hot oil. Fry in batches for about 3 minutes or until crisp and golden brown. Remove with a slotted spoon when they are ready, and drain on paper towels.
3 Serve the pakoras as soon as they are done, with the chutney. **SERVES 4**

Lime, mirin, and tamari dressing

A light, tangy dressing that is ideal with firm fish such as tuna, marlin or swordfish. The lime juice acts as the perfect foil for the mirin, which is sweeter than sake and only used for cooking.

Katsuo is the Japanese word for bonito, a close relative of the Mediterranean tuna which only grows to 3 or 4 feet long. The cooking time for the tuna in this recipe will depend on the thickness of the steak and how rare you like your fish. On average, allow about 1 to 2 minutes each side in a heavy skillet over brisk heat. A cast-iron ridged stovetop grill pan works well, but make sure the pan is really hot before you add the tuna, or the steaks will stick.

Whisk the ingredients together until evenly combined.

Finely grated rind and juice of 2 limes
1 tsp (5 mL) fresh ginger purée
2 tbsp (25 mL) mirin
4 tbsp (50 mL) tamari soy sauce

Katsuo tataki SEARED TUNA WITH SHREDDED VEGETABLE SALAD

1 Peel the daikon and carrots. Julienne the daikon, carrots and zucchini into long, spaghetti-like strips using a mandoline, food processor attachment, or sharp knife. Blanch in a pan of boiling water for 2 minutes or until starting to soften.
2 Heat the oil in a heavy skillet and when very hot, add the tuna steaks and cook for 1 to 2 minutes each side or until done to your liking.
3 Drain the vegetables and toss with half the mint and the sesame seeds. Divide between serving plates and top with the tuna steaks. Spoon the dressing over the steaks and serve garnished with the reserved mint.
SERVES 4

10½ oz (300 g) daikon (white radish)
2 medium carrots
1 yellow zucchini
2 tbsp (25 mL) vegetable oil
4 tuna steaks
2 tbsp (25 mL) finely chopped mint
1 tsp (5 mL) black sesame seeds
1 quantity Lime, Mirin, and
   Tamari Dressing

VARIATION The recipe can also be made with other oily fish fillets such as mackerel or salmon.

Fish sauce, herb, and lime dressing

2 tbsp (25 mL) nam pla (Thai fish sauce)

2 cloves garlic, peeled and minced

1 tbsp (15 mL) rice vinegar

Juice of 1 lime

1 tsp (5 mL) soft brown sugar

2 tbsp (25 mL) chopped fresh cilantro

2 tbsp (25 mL) chopped mint

A hot and sour mix used to dress a spicy salad of broiled beef on a bed of fresh seasonal vegetables and salad leaves. Pour the dressing over the salad and toss the ingredients together just before serving.

Because the beef in Yum nua is only lightly cooked, it must be as tender as possible, so sirloin, rump, and fillet steak are the best cuts to use. Trim any fat from the steak before broiling, and after broiling allow it to stand for 10 minutes so it is easier to carve into very thin slices. A cast-iron ridged grill pan is recommended because it can be heated to a sufficiently high temperature to seal the meat and ensure that it stays tender, but a conventional broiler could be used as well.

Place the ingredients in a covered container and shake well or whisk together in a bowl until combined and the sugar has dissolved.

Yum nua GRILLED THAI BEEF SALAD

1 lb (450 g) fillet or thick sirloin
    steak in one piece

2 tbsp (25 mL) peanut oil

3½ oz (100 g) arugula (mizuna) leaves

1 small red onion, peeled and finely sliced

6 cherry tomatoes, halved

½ cucumber, julienned

1 quantity Fish Sauce, Herb, and
    Lime Dressing

GARNISH WITH

1 red chile, seeded and finely chopped

1 Brush the steak with the oil and cook in a grill pan over high heat until well-browned but still pink in the center. Alternatively, broil the meat under high heat and set aside for 10 minutes, reserving any juices that have come out of the meat.

2 Arrange the arugula, onion, tomato halves, and cucumber on a serving dish. With a sharp knife, slice the steak as thinly as possible and place the slices on top of the salad leaves and vegetables. Whisk any meat juices into the dressing and spoon over the salad.

3 Toss lightly and serve sprinkled with the finely chopped chile. SERVES 4

VARIATION Broiled chicken breasts can be used to make the salad but must be cooked thoroughly first.

Fresh cilantro, lime, and green chile dressing

Known in Thailand as nam jim, this is an all-purpose salad dressing. The proportion and mix of ingredients varies according to the cook who is making it and the locality. The Thais use the whole cilantro plant in cooking, so buy a bunch of leaves with its roots attached and save the sprigs to use as a garnish in another recipe. The dressing should be neither too salty nor too sweet and the garlic should not be too dominant, so adjust the balance of ingredients if necessary.

This simple chicken salad contains pomelo, a large yellow-green citrus fruit similar to a grapefruit but with a crunchier, flakier flesh. To prepare, peel, separate into wedges, and then pull off the papery skin that encloses each segment of flesh. In Thailand, pomelo is eaten as a fruit or mixed with sweet-sour ingredients in a salad.

1 clove garlic, peeled and sliced
2 fresh cilantro roots, washed and dried
½ green chile, seeded
About ⅔ cup (150 mL) fresh lime juice
2 tsp (10 mL) soft light brown sugar
2 tsp (10 mL) nam pla (Thai fish sauce)

Coarsely blend the garlic and fresh cilantro in a spice mill or pound in a mortar and pestle. Add the chiles and blend or pound again, then work in the lime juice. Add the sugar and fish sauce, and stir until the sugar dissolves.

Yam som-o CHICKEN AND POMELO SALAD

1 Peel the pomelo, divide into segments, and remove the papery skin. Break up the flesh into chunks.
2 Place in a bowl, add the dressing and stir to mix. Add the shrimp, chicken and grated coconut and toss lightly together.
3 Spoon into a serving dish and garnish with fresh cilantro leaves. SERVES 4

VARIATIONS Instead of chicken, use cubes of cooked white fish or baby squid mixed with the shrimp.

1 pomelo (or use two grapefruit)
1 quantity Fresh Cilantro, Lime, and Green Chile Dressing
6 oz (175 g) cooked, peeled shrimp
12 oz (350 g) cooked chicken, shredded
3 tbsp (45 mL) grated fresh coconut

GARNISH WITH

Fresh cilantro leaves

Lemongrass, cilantro, and ginger dressing

½ tsp (2 mL) fresh lemongrass purée

1 tsp (5 mL) fresh ginger purée

1 tbsp (15 mL) chopped fresh cilantro

2 tbsp (25 mL) nam pla (Thai fish sauce)

1 tbsp (15 mL) chopped mint

Juice of 2 limes

1 tsp (5 mL) soft light brown sugar

2 red chiles, seeded and finely chopped

Salads are an important part of any Thai meal and, in common with other dishes, the basic flavors of sour, sweet, hot, and savory are carefully balanced. These flavors come through in the dressings, which can be laden with chiles or not, as the diner prefers.

The Thais use only the freshest ingredients to make their salads and most people will shop early at their local market before the sun has had a chance to wilt the delicate produce. Green papaya salad is one of the most popular; street vendors are constantly pounding and preparing the ingredients so the salads can always be freshly made. A "green" papaya is one that is slightly underripe so the salad is not too sweet and soft. It should be prepared just before serving so the papaya does not lose its firm texture.

Mix all the ingredients together.

2 tbsp (25 mL) peanut oil

1 shallot, peeled and finely chopped

1 garlic clove, peeled and minced

9 oz (250 g) finely ground pork

1 tsp (5 mL) ground coriander

2 tbsp (25 mL) light soy sauce

9 oz (250 g) unripe green papaya, seeded, peeled and cut into matchsticks

1 quantity Lemongrass, Cilantro, and Ginger Dressing

1 mango, peeled and chopped

4 cherry tomatoes, halved or quartered

GARNISH WITH

Fresh cilantro leaves

Yam mamuang GREEN PAPAYA SALAD WITH PORK AND MANGO

1 Heat the oil in a skillet, add the shallot, and fry for 5 minutes. Stir in the garlic, pork and coriander and stir over fairly brisk heat for a couple of minutes until the pork starts to brown. Add the soy sauce and cook, stirring occasionally, until the sauce has been absorbed by the meat and the pork is quite dry. Remove from the heat and set aside.

2 Using a mortar and pestle pound the papaya with 2 tablespoons of the dressing or blend to a coarse purée in a food processor. Spoon into a serving dish, top with the warm pork, mango, and tomatoes and pour over the rest of the dressing. Serve garnished with fresh cilantro leaves. SERVES 4

VARIATIONS Chicken pieces, small shrimp, or strips of seared steak can be stir-fried in place of the pork.

Lemongrass dressing

⅔ cup (150 mL) water

1 tbsp (15 mL) nam pla (Thai fish sauce)

½ tsp (2 mL) shrimp paste

1 tbsp (15 mL) soft brown sugar

1 tsp (5 mL) fresh lemongrass purée

Finely grated rind and juice of 1 lime

1 tbsp (15 mL) finely torn basil (Thai,
   if available)

Thai salads are hot and sour and use lots of fresh herbs such as mint, fresh cilantro, Chinese chive and Thai basil. The basil (horapha) has deep-green, oval-shaped leaves with purple stems running through them, is stronger in flavor than the Mediterranean variety, and has a strong perfume of aniseed.

   This recipe is a useful way to use up leftover cooked Thai fragrant rice. The ingredients for the salad are arranged on serving plates around a mound of rice in the center so that diners can take a little of each ingredient and mix it with the rice as they wish. Dried shrimp are available from Thai food stores.

Place the water in a saucepan and add the fish sauce, shrimp paste, sugar, lemongrass purée, lime rind, and juice and bring to a boil. Simmer for 2 minutes, then remove from the heat and add the basil.

3 tbsp (45 mL) dried shrimp

2 large eggs, beaten

1 lb (450 g) cold cooked rice

1 underripe (green) mango, peeled and
   the flesh sliced away from the pit

4 oz (100 g) bean sprouts

4 oz (100 g) cooked green beans, sliced

4 tbsp (50 mL) shaved fresh coconut
   flesh, lightly toasted

4 oz (100 g) cooked, peeled shrimp

1 slice pineapple, cut into small pieces

1 quantity Lemongrass Dressing

GARNISH WITH

Lime wedges, fresh cilantro sprigs,
   chopped red chiles

Khao yam paak tai RICE, MANGO, AND SHRIMP SALAD

1 Place the dried shrimp in a bowl, cover with boiling water, and allow to soak for 10 minutes, then drain. Make a thin omelet of the eggs (for method see Stir-fried Chicken with Shredded Omelet, page 34). Remove from the pan, roll up, and slice thinly.

2 Divide the rice into four cups or small basins, press down to shape the rice, and turn the mounds out into the center of four large serving plates.

3 Arrange the soaked dried shrimp, sliced omelet, mango, bean sprouts, beans, coconut, shrimp, and pineapple in separate mounds around the rice and spoon the dressing over them. Garnish with lime wedges, fresh cilantro sprigs, and chopped red chiles.

4 To serve, give each diner a small plate so they can take a little rice and mix with a selection of individual ingredients. Serve the dressing separately, if preferred. **SERVES 4**

VARIATIONS The salad ingredients around the rice can be varied according to what is available. Underripe papaya, pomelo segments, tomato wedges, baby corn or cooked shredded chicken would all be appropriate.

4 Dipping sauces and relishes

Small bowls of piquant dipping sauces and relishes are served alongside many dishes at Asian meals to temper the richness of fried foods, to enhance a plainly broiled meat kebob, or simply to add additional flavor to vegetables, seafood and bean curd. Each country's dipping sauces tend to mirror the favorite flavors of its national cuisine. In China this might be sweet and sour with hoi sin and soy, in Thailand a fiery mix based on chiles, while in Korea dips will be fragrant with the aroma of toasted sesame. In Japan, dips are delicate and subtly flavored, as with most Japanese sauces, with light soy sauce, sake, and mirin. The unsuspecting, however, should beware of the wasabi that is often served alongside. Pale green and swirled in a decorative cone, this is Japan's fiercely hot horseradish and not for the faint-hearted!

4 tbsp (50 mL) plum sauce, bought
  or homemade
1 tbsp (15 mL) light soy sauce
¼ tsp (1 mL) sweet chile sauce
1 garlic clove, peeled and minced

14 oz (400 g) raw medium-sized shrimp,
  shelled and coarsely chopped
1 slice ham, chopped
4 scallions, chopped
1 egg white, lightly beaten
1 tsp (5 mL) finely grated gingerroot
2 tsp (10 mL) light soy sauce
1 tsp (5 mL) sugar
1 tsp (5 mL) sesame oil
Salt and pepper
6 large thin slices white bread,
  crusts removed
3 tbsp (45 mL) sesame seeds
Peanut oil for deep-frying
Chopped green onions, to garnish

SERVE WITH

1 quantity Plum Dipping Sauce

Plum dipping sauce

Bottled plum sauces can be bought in Oriental food stores and larger supermarkets or you can use the plum sauce recipe given on page 30. Plum blossom is the Chinese national emblem in the same way that cherry blossom symbolizes Japan.

Although not Chinese in origin, sesame shrimp toasts are served as an appetizer in almost every Chinese restaurant in the West as well as many restaurants in China. They also make a popular party hors d'oeuvre when handed round on trays with drinks. The paste can be prepared ahead and kept in a covered bowl in the refrigerator, but the toasts should only be cooked just before serving. Allow them to cool a little after frying, so guests do not burn their mouths.

Stir the ingredients together until combined.

Zhima xia tushi SESAME SHRIMP TOASTS

1 Place the shrimp, ham, and scallions in a food processor and blend to a paste. Transfer to a bowl and stir in the egg white, ginger, soy sauce, sugar, and sesame oil. Add salt and pepper to taste.
2 Cut each slice of bread into four squares. Spread the shrimp paste quite thickly on the bread squares and sprinkle with the sesame seeds.
3 Heat the oil in a wok or large pan to 350°F (180°C) and deep-fry the toasts three or four at a time, paste-side down for 2 minutes, then turn them over and fry for a further 2 minutes or until golden brown and crisp.
4 Remove with a slotted spoon, drain on paper towels, and serve warm with the Plum Dipping Sauce. Garnish with chopped green onions. **MAKES 24**

VARIATIONS Add two minced bacon slices to the shrimp paste instead of the ham, and two finely chopped shallots instead of the scallions.

Sweet soy sauce

2 tbsp (25 mL) Chinese light soy sauce

2 tbsp (25 mL) rice vinegar

1 tbsp (15 mL) dark soft brown sugar

1 scallion, trimmed and finely sliced

1 tsp (5 mL) sesame seeds

The Indonesians use a thick, syrupy soy sauce called kecap manis, and lighter sweet soy sauces are used by the Japanese. This sauce is based on light Chinese soy sauce, which is made from the juice of the first pressing of the fermented soy beans, whereas Chinese dark soy sauce is a blend of subsequent pressings of the beans to which caramel is added to give the sauce a darker color.

Dim sum is the umbrella name for small snacks. The Cantonese like to have them for breakfast, while in other parts of China (and also in Canton), they are eaten between mid-morning and late afternoon accompanied by a bottomless pot of tea. Dim sum translates literally as "snacks to eat for pleasure" and dozens of different varieties are available in the huge dim sum restaurants in Hong Kong and Canton. Among the most popular dim sum are steamed buns filled with barbecued pork (chao siu), deep-fried wontons, spring rolls, spareribs, sesame shrimp toasts, and these small dumplings called haw gow stuffed with ground pork and shrimp.

Stir the soy sauce, vinegar, and sugar together until the sugar dissolves. Add the scallion and sesame seeds.

Dim sum

9 oz (250 g) ground pork

4½ oz (125 g) small peeled shrimp, coarsely chopped

3 oz (75 g) bok choy, stalk removed and leaves finely shredded

2 shallots, peeled and finely chopped

1 tsp (5 mL) sesame oil

2 tsp (10 mL) light soy sauce

24 wonton wrappers

SERVE WITH

1 quantity Sweet Soy Sauce

1 Mix together the pork, shrimp, bok choy, shallots, sesame oil, and soy sauce in a bowl until evenly combined.

2 Place a teaspoon of the mixture in the center of a wonton wrapper. Dampen the edges and fold one point diagonally over the filling to the point opposite and press together. Lift up the point, then dampen the two side points and overlap them on top, pinching together. Repeat with the rest of the wrappers and filling.

3 Cook the dumplings in a Chinese bamboo steamer set over a wok or a large saucepan of boiling water or thinned chicken stock for 6 to 7 minutes or until translucent.

4 Serve with the sauce. **MAKES 24**

VARIATIONS Use young spinach leaves or Chinese cabbage instead of bok choy. The dumplings can be deep-fried until crisp and golden if preferred.

Pon-zu

Half soy sauce and half freshly squeezed citrus juice, Pon-zu is served as a dressing or dipping sauce for broiled meat and seafood. The dashi stock used can be the one given on page 111 or can be made with purchased granules or powder.

Teppanyaki is the Japanese method of cooking meat on a flat metal plate. As steak houses opened in the West in the sixties and seventies, Japan opened its own teppan restaurants in a bid to attract tourists. The restaurants, where customers sit around a large central grill with a chef cooking sizzling chunks of tender beef and vegetables to order, proved popular with the Japanese as well. These days, seafood and chicken may also be added to the hot plate as well, but prime beef from Matsuzaka and Kobe is still the main attraction. As few private homes will have the type of grill plate used in Japanese restaurants, the beef can be cooked on a cast-iron, stovetop grill pan.

Mix the lime juice, soy sauce, and dashi in a small bowl and add the sliced onions and daikon.

- 4 tbsp (50 mL) freshly squeezed lime juice
- 4 tbsp (50 mL) Japanese soy sauce
- 4 tbsp (50 mL) dashi stock
- 2 scallions (green tops only), finely sliced
- 2 tsp (10 mL) grated daikon (white radish)

Teppanyaki JAPANESE SEARED BEEF

1 Place the beef in a bowl, cover with the soy sauce and mirin, and sprinkle with the ginger and garlic. Stir until the beef is coated, then allow to stand for 15 minutes.
2 Toss the mushrooms in half the oil.
3 Heat a grill pan until very hot and prepare with the remaining oil. Cook the beef and vegetables in batches over high heat, until the beef is well browned and done to your liking and the vegetables are just tender.
4 Serve with the Pon-zu dipping sauce. **SERVES 4**

VARIATIONS If using chicken, use breast meat, skinned and cut into strips across the grain of the meat. For shrimp, use raw jumbo shrimp that have been peeled and deveined.

- 1¼ lb (675 g) beef fillet, thinly sliced into strips
- 3 tbsp (45 mL) Japanese soy sauce
- 1 tbsp (15 mL) mirin
- 1 tsp (5 mL) grated gingerroot
- 2 cloves garlic, peeled and minced
- 8 shiitake mushrooms
- 2 tbsp (25 mL) peanut oil
- 1 red bell pepper, seeded and sliced
- 2 oz (50 g) snow peas, sliced
- 1 red onion, cut into 8 wedges and layers separated
- 5 oz (150 g) bean sprouts

SERVE WITH

- 1 quantity Pon-zu

Light soy and mirin dipping sauce

Mirin is a sweet rice wine that is added to rice when making sushi and is also a common ingredient in dipping sauces and marinades. Japanese flavors are strong yet subtle, so the soy sauce used for this recipe is smoother and milder than a fuller-flavored soy sauce such as kecap manis from Indonesia.

Although now one of Japan's most popular dishes, tempura only became part of the country's cuisine in the 16th century when it was introduced by the Portuguese. The batter should be made just before use and the fried vegetables eaten immediately so they remain crisp and light.

1 To make the dashi stock, place the kelp in the water and bring just to a boil. As soon as the water boils, remove the kelp. Add the bonito flakes, without stirring, and return to a boil. Remove the saucepan from the heat. When the bonito flakes sink, the stock is ready.
2 Strain the stock through a fine sieve. The reserved kelp and drained bonito flakes can be used again, although subsequent stocks will have a less-concentrated flavor.
3 Bring the stock back to a boil and add the soy sauce and mirin. Remove from the heat.

BASIC DASHI STOCK

2-in (5-cm) strip dried kelp
1 cup (225 mL) water
½ oz (15 g) dried bonito flakes

3 tbsp (45 mL) light soy sauce
3 tbsp (45 mL) mirin

Tempura vegetables

1 To make the batter put the egg yolks in a bowl and mix in the water. Beat until frothy. Add the flour and beat until just combined. The batter should be the consistency of light cream, so if it is too thick add a few extra drops of iced water.
2 Prepare and blanch the vegetables as needed and set them out on a plate or tray ready for cooking.
3 When ready to serve, heat the oil in a deep saucepan to 375°F (190°C). Using chopsticks, dip the vegetable pieces in the batter one at a time and drop into the oil, frying about six pieces at a time.
4 Fry for about 2 to 4 minutes until the batter turns golden, then remove and drain thoroughly on paper towels.
5 Reheat the Light Soy and Mirin Dipping Sauce and pour into a bowl. Serve at once with the tempura. **SERVES 4**

VARIATIONS Strips of firm fish such as sole, flounder, or monkfish and large, raw, deveined shrimp can be dipped in the batter and fried in the same way. The dipping sauce is also excellent served with seafood, as it brings out the subtler flavors.

BATTER

2 egg yolks
1 cup (225 mL) iced water
1⅔ cups (200 mL) all-purpose
   flour, sifted

2 lb (900 g) vegetables, e.g., carrots,
   zucchini, cauliflower florets,
   mushrooms, baby corn, prepared as
   necessary, blanched and julienned or
   cut into bite-sized pieces
Vegetable oil for deep-frying
1 quantity Light Soy and Mirin Dipping
   Sauce

Sesame dipping sauce

1 tbsp (15 mL) white sesame seeds

4 tbsp (50 mL) light soy sauce

¼ tsp (1 mL) ngapi (dried shrimp paste)

1 tbsp (15 mL) white wine vinegar

½ tsp (2 mL) sugar

1 small red chile, seeded and chopped

Although cutlery is also used today, Burmese food was traditionally eaten with the fingers. A popular way to start a meal is to offer a selection of small dishes, known locally as tolee molee or "bits and pieces." Burmese cuisine does not use a large selection of spices: garlic, chiles, turmeric, and ginger are the seasonings most commonly used. Inevitably, the amount of chile added will govern the "heat" of a dish. Ngapi is Myanmar's version of dried shrimp paste and it is one of the characteristic flavors of the country's cuisine.

Beya kyaw is one of the small dishes that might be served at the start of a Burmese meal. Soak the split peas for at least 12 hours or overnight before cooking.

Toast the sesame seeds in a dry, heavy skillet until just golden. Remove immediately from the pan and mix with the soy sauce, shrimp paste, vinegar, and sugar, stirring until the sugar dissolves. Serve in a small bowl, sprinkled with the chile.

Beya kyaw SPLIT PEA FRITTERS

1 cup (225 mL) yellow split peas

1 tbsp (15 mL) besan (chickpea flour)
   or all-purpose whole-wheat flour

1 small onion, peeled and very finely
   chopped

½ tsp (2 mL) turmeric

1 garlic clove, peeled and minced

½ tsp (2 mL) chili powder

1 tsp (5 mL) baking powder

Salt and pepper

Vegetable or peanut oil for deep-frying

SERVE WITH

1 quantity Sesame Dipping Sauce

1 Place the split peas in a bowl, cover with cold water, and soak for 12 hours or overnight. Drain.

2 Grind the split peas in a food processor to a fine meal. Transfer to a bowl and stir in the flour, onion, turmeric, garlic, chili, baking powder, and seasoning. Beat until the mixture is light and fluffy.

3 Heat oil for deep-frying in a wok or large pan to 375°F (190°C). Roll the mixture into walnut-sized balls and fry in two or three batches until golden brown.

4 Drain on paper towels and serve warm with the Sesame Dipping Sauce.

SERVES 4

VARIATION Add 2 tablespoons chopped fresh cilantro to the fritter mixture.

Garlic, chile, and lime dipping sauce

1 tsp (5 mL) sugar

1 tbsp (15 mL) fresh lime juice

2 tbsp (25 mL) nuoc mam (Vietnamese fish sauce)

1 tsp (5 mL) rice vinegar

6 tbsp (75 mL) water or juice from a fresh coconut

2 cloves garlic, peeled and minced

1 red chile, seeded and finely sliced

Known as nuoc cham and made by mixing garlic, chile, vinegar, sugar, and lime juice with the Vietnamese fish sauce nuoc mam. Vietnam's fish sauce is brewed all along the country's coastal and delta regions and is produced from small, anchovy-like fish that are layered with salt and left to ferment in barrels for up to three months. The resulting liquid is drained off through a tap at the bottom of the barrel, poured back in, left for a further three months, and then drained off again. The liquid is strained ready for sale or, like fine wine, aged further so that its flavor will improve over the years.

Nem nuong is another popular street food in Vietnam, where vendors barbecue these spicy meatballs, usually made of pork, on skewers over charcoal. The fat from the meat drips down over the coals and the resulting smoke adds its own irresistible aroma. The meatballs can be dipped straight into the nuoc cham sauce or pulled off their skewers and wrapped in crisp lettuce leaves first.

Stir the sugar into the lime juice, fish sauce, vinegar, and water or coconut juice until it dissolves. Add the garlic and chile.

Nem nuong SPICY BARBECUED MEATBALLS

1 lb 2 oz (500 g) ground pork

2 cloves garlic, peeled and minced

1 tsp (5 mL) fresh ginger purée

2 tbsp (25 mL) nuoc mam (Vietnamese fish sauce)

1 tsp (5 mL) fresh lemongrass purée

Juice of 1 lime

2 tsp (10 mL) sugar

1 small green chile, seeded and finely chopped

SERVE WITH

4 tbsp (50 mL) unsalted peanuts, roasted and finely chopped

Matchsticks of cucumber, carrot, and daikon (white radish)

Fresh cilantro and mint sprigs

1 quantity Chile, Garlic, and Lime Dipping Sauce (nuoc cham)

1 Put the ground pork in a bowl and break up with a fork. Add the garlic, ginger purée, fish sauce, lemongrass purée, lime juice, sugar, and chile. Stir well until mixed. Set aside for 30 minutes.

2 Soak 12 bamboo skewers in cold water for 30 minutes.

3 Roll the pork mixture into small balls and thread onto the skewers. Barbecue or broil for 7 to 8 minutes, turning frequently until the meatballs are browned and cooked through.

4 Arrange on a platter and sprinkle with the peanuts. Arrange the cucumber, carrot and daikon alongside, garnish with fresh cilantro and mint sprigs, and serve with the Chile, Garlic, and Lime Dipping Sauce. **SERVES 4**

VARIATION Use lean pork steaks cut into cubes or strips and threaded onto the skewers. As the meat cooks, brush with any marinade left in the bowl.

Yellow bean and peanut dipping sauce

Nuoc thuon, or Vietnamese yellow bean sauce, is available ready-made from Oriental food stores and can be used to make this dipping sauce. It is traditionally served with spicy beef threaded onto skewers for broiling. When they are done, they are pulled off the skewers, wrapped in lettuce leaves, and dipped in the sauce.

In Hanoi these delicious broiled beef rolls are often known as boeuf Napoléon, although apart from the country's French colonial heritage the precise derivation of the name is unclear. The beef is sliced very thinly and marinated in spices before being broiled on skewers. When done, the meat is pushed off the skewer onto a lettuce leaf and fresh cilantro, scallion, cucumber, and bean sprouts are added. The leaf is then wrapped around the beef and the roll dipped in Yellow Bean and Peanut Dipping Sauce.

Mix the ingredients together until well blended.

1 cup (225 mL) yellow bean sauce
  (nuoc thuon)*

4 tbsp (50 mL) chile sauce or to taste

1 tbsp (15 mL) ground, unsalted, roasted
  peanuts

Banh uot thit nuong BROILED BEEF ROLLS

1 Put the lemongrass, shallots, pepper, chili powder, salt, pepper, and half the oil in a food processor and blend to a paste. Heat the remaining oil in a skillet, add the paste and fry for 5 minutes. Allow to cool.

2 Cut the steak into thin slices and place in a dish. Spread the paste and any oil in the pan over the meat, turning it until coated. Cover and leave in a cool place for several hours or overnight.

3 Thread the meat onto skewers and broil for about 6 to 8 minutes or until done to your liking, turning over once.

5 To serve, push a few pieces of steak off a skewer onto a lettuce leaf, add mint or fresh cilantro sprigs, a little shredded scallion, chopped cucumber and a few bean sprouts, and roll the leaf around the filling. Dip the parcel in the sauce before eating. **SERVES 4**

1 stalk lemongrass, finely chopped

6 shallots, peeled and chopped

½ red bell pepper, seeded and chopped

¼ tsp (1 mL) chili powder

½ tsp (2 mL) salt

½ tsp (2 mL) ground black pepper

4 tbsp (50 mL) vegetable oil

1 lb 2 oz (500 g) sirloin steak

SERVE WITH

Lettuce leaves, mint or fresh cilantro
  sprigs, shredded scallion, chopped
  cucumber, bean sprouts

1 quantity Yellow Bean and Peanut
  Dipping Sauce

VARIATION Pork may be used instead of beef.

*TO MAKE YOUR OWN YELLOW BEAN SAUCE In a food processor, blend 9 oz (250 g) cooked yellow soy beans with 2 tbsp (25 mL) coconut milk, 2 tbsp (25 mL) ground unsalted roasted peanuts, 2 tsp (10 mL) sugar, 3 minced cloves garlic, 1 seeded finely chopped medium red chile, and 1 stalk finely chopped lemongrass. Fry the mixture in 2 tbsp (25 mL) vegetable oil for 2 minutes.

3 cloves garlic, chopped

2 tbsp (25 mL) chopped shallots

1 tbsp (15 mL) vegetable oil

1 small carrot, finely diced

1 small red bell pepper, seeded
   and finely diced

1 red chile, seeded and sliced

1 tbsp (15 mL) sugar

Salt and pepper

1 tsp (5 mL) tomato ketchup

2 tbsp (25 mL) rice vinegar

2 tsp (10 mL) cornstarch

9 oz (250 g) raw shrimp, peeled and
   minced

Salt and pepper to taste

1 tsp (5 mL) sugar

1 green chile, seeded and finely chopped

8 4-in (10-cm) sugar cane sticks, peeled,
   or lemongrass stalks

2 tbsp (25 mL) vegetable oil

1 quantity Sweet and Sour Chile
   Dipping Sauce

GARNISH WITH

Fresh cilantro sprigs

Sweet and sour chile dipping sauce

Modern Vietnamese cuisine is the fusion of traditional Chinese cooking with European ingredients and techniques, a legacy of the years of French rule in Indochina.

Chao tom is a classic dish from the Imperial City of Hue which uses pieces of sugar cane as skewers. Syrup seeping from the hot cane flavors the shrimp mixture when you bite into it. If you can't get hold of sugar cane, use lemongrass stalks instead.

Fry the garlic and shallots gently in the oil until golden. Add the carrot, red bell pepper, chile, sugar, and seasoning to taste. Fry for 5 minutes then add the tomato ketchup and vinegar. Blend the cornstarch with a little cold water and stir into the sauce. Simmer for a further 1 minute.

Chao tom SHRIMP ON SUGAR CANE WITH SWEET AND SOUR SAUCE

1 Season the minced shrimp with salt and pepper then stir in the sugar and chile. Divide into eight and mold each portion around a stick of sugar cane or a lemongrass stalk. Place on a foil-lined broiler rack and brush with the oil.
2 Broil under medium heat for about 5 minutes or until the shrimp mixture is firm and opaque, turning the skewers over once or twice.
3 Serve with the warm sauce for dipping and garnish with fresh cilantro sprigs. SERVES 4

VARIATIONS Serve the the Sweet and Sour Chile Dipping Sauce as a dip for barbecued chicken wings, crumb- or batter-coated fish goujons (scampi-sized pieces), and grilled tofu and vegetable kebobs.

Rice vinegar, basil, and chile dipping sauce

2 tbsp (25 mL) fish sauce

Juice of 1 lime

1 tbsp (15 mL) sugar

1 garlic clove, peeled and minced

1 tbsp (15 mL) rice vinegar

4 tbsp (50 mL) water

1 red chile, seeded and very finely chopped

1 tsp (5 mL) chopped fresh basil

Vietnamese food is characterized by its fresh, lively flavors and this tangy dipping sauce is one that would typically be served with their delicate rice rolls, wafer-thin white wrappers made with rice flour and filled with anything from ground meat and shellfish to fried bean curd (tofu), green leaves and vegetables.

The Vietnamese spring roll wrappers needed for this recipe are small translucent rice flour pancakes, available dried in packages from larger supermarkets and Oriental food stores. They just need to be dampened slightly or dipped in hot water to make them soft enough to roll. These are a favorite street food in Vietnam, where the wrappers are filled to order with the customers' chosen ingredients. Straw mushrooms can be bought in cans but if they are unavailable, use another Asian variety such as shiitake or enoki.

Stir the fish sauce, lime juice, sugar, garlic, vinegar, and water together until the sugar dissolves. Sprinkle in the chile and basil.

Banh cuon VIETNAMESE RICE ROLLS

2 tbsp (25 mL) peanut oil

1 large carrot, peeled and cut into matchsticks

4 shallots, peeled and sliced

3 oz (75 g) daikon (white radish), peeled and cut into matchsticks

4 oz (100 g) straw mushrooms, chopped

8 oz (250 g) firm tofu (bean curd), cut into matchsticks

2 tbsp (25 mL) light soy sauce

1 tsp (5 mL) sesame oil

Small bunch fresh cilantro sprigs

12 rice flour pancakes

SERVE WITH

1 quantity Rice Vinegar, Basil, and Chile Dipping Sauce

1 Heat the oil in a wok, add the carrot and shallots, and stir-fry for 2 minutes. Add the daikon, straw mushrooms, and tofu and stir-fry for 5 minutes. Add the soy sauce, sesame oil and fresh cilantro, and remove from the heat.

2 Dip one rice flour pancake in hot water for a few seconds until soft enough to roll. Place on a board and spoon some of the filling on one half. Wrap the pancake around the tofu mixture and roll to make a cone. Repeat with the remaining pancakes and filling.

3 Serve with the dipping sauce. SERVES 4

VARIATIONS Substitute chopped shrimp or lean pork, ground or finely chopped, for the tofu.

Sweet chile dipping sauce

Sweet chile sauce is the usual condiment served with snacks sold at street food stalls in Thailand. It is packaged in small plastic bags for dipping on the go, or for pouring over a more leisurely sit-down snack.

These tiny, bite-sized Thai fish cakes make an excellent snack to serve with drinks or as an appetizer. In this recipe, salmon and white fish are mixed with spices and lime leaves, but different combinations of fish can be used. Lime is an important flavoring so if you cannot find fresh lime leaves, use the finely grated rind of two limes instead.

½ cup (125 mL) rice vinegar
½ cup (125 mL) sugar
3 large, long red chiles, seeded
¼ cucumber, peeled, seeded, and grated

1 Put the vinegar and sugar in a saucepan and heat gently until the sugar dissolves. Add the chiles and simmer for 10 minutes. Remove from the heat and allow to cool.
2 Purée in a blender or food processor. Stir in the grated cucumber.

Taud mun THAI FISH CAKES

1 Cut the salmon and white fish into chunks and place in a food processor with the ginger purée, lemongrass purée, and lime leaves. Process until coarsely ground.
2 Transfer to a bowl and stir in the fish sauce, green beans, fresh cilantro, and egg white.
3 Shape into small balls and then flatten into cakes ½-in (1-cm) thick. Shallow-fry in hot oil for 2 minutes each side until golden and done. Drain on paper towels and serve with lime wedges and the dipping sauce.
MAKES ABOUT 20

VARIATIONS Use all white fish rather than a mix of white and salmon, or replace some of the fish with white crabmeat, prepared squid or raw medium-sized shrimp.

8 oz (225 g) salmon fillet, skinned
8 oz (225 g) firm white fish fillet, e.g., flounder, sole, or monkfish, skinned
1 tsp (5 mL) fresh ginger purée
1 tsp (5 mL) fresh lemongrass purée
2 kaffir lime leaves, very finely shredded
1 tbsp (15 mL) nam pla (Thai fish sauce)
4 oz (100 g) fine green beans, trimmed and finely chopped
1 tbsp (15 mL) chopped fresh cilantro
1 egg white, lightly beaten
Oil for shallow-frying

SERVE WITH

Lime wedges
1 quantity Sweet Chile Dipping Sauce

Chile preserve

There are probably as many recipes in Thailand for chile preserve as there are cooks but the common ingredient in all of them is the large dried red chiles available from Thai food stores or other Oriental food shops. Fresh chiles will not give the same intense flavor and color and their extra fluid will prevent the preserve from becoming thick and sticky.

Adding yeast to the batter mix in this recipe gives fish a wonderfully crisp, light coating that will not go soggy after frying. To activate the yeast effectively, it is important to stir it thoroughly into the flour before adding the liquid.

1 Place the chiles in a bowl, cover with hot water and leave to soak for 30 minutes. Drain, split open and remove the seeds.
2 Heat oil for deep-frying in a wok and deep-fry the chiles for a couple of minutes until they are dark red. Drain on paper towels.
3 Remove all but 2 tablespoons of the oil and fry the bell pepper and shallots for 5 minutes. Add the garlic, fry for 2 minutes, then stir in the tomatoes, chiles, and shrimp paste.
4 Lower the heat and simmer gently for 30 minutes. Cool a little, then purée in a food processor with the sugar and fish sauce.
5 Return the purée to the wok and cook it very gently for about 40 minutes until dark, caramelized and jelly-like in consistency, stirring regularly so it does not stick to the pan and burn. **MAKES ABOUT 1 ½ CUPS (350 ML)**

½ oz (15 g) large dried red chiles
Peanut oil for deep-frying
1 red bell pepper, seeded and chopped
4 purple shallots, peeled and chopped
2 cloves garlic, peeled and chopped
8-fl oz (225-mL) can chopped tomatoes
1 tsp (5 mL) shrimp paste
2 tbsp (25 mL) soft brown sugar
¼ cup (100 mL) nam pla (Thai fish sauce)

Pra tod lard prik CRISP FRIED FISH WITH CHILE PRESERVE

1 Sprinkle the yeast and sugar over the flour in a bowl and stir well. Add the water and mix with a wooden spoon to make a smooth batter. Cover and leave for 1 hour until frothy.
2 Heat oil for deep-frying in a wok or large saucepan to 375°F (190°C). Stir the fresh cilantro into the batter.
3 Coat the fish pieces in seasoned flour and dip in the batter until coated. Fry a few pieces at a time in the hot oil for about 5 minutes or until golden brown and crisp. Drain on paper towels and keep warm while you fry the rest.
4 Serve the fish with a little of the Chile Preserve, garnished with wedges of lime for squeezing over the fish. **SERVES 4**

VARIATION Can be prepared with any firm white fish. If using a flat fish such as sole or flounder, cut the fillets into fairly wide strips and reduce the frying time to 2 to 3 minutes.

¼-oz (7-g) package dry yeast
Pinch sugar
¾ cup (175 mL) all-purpose flour, plus
    extra seasoned flour to coat the fish
⅔ cup (150 mL) tepid water
Peanut or vegetable oil for deep-frying
1 tbsp (15 mL) chopped fresh cilantro
1¼ lb (550 g) firm white fish fillets, e.g.,
    monkfish, sea bass, or cod, cut into
    2-in (5-cm) pieces

SERVE WITH

Chile Preserve
Lime wedges

Vinegar dipping sauce

6 tbsp (75 mL) Japanese soy sauce

2 tbsp (25 mL) rice vinegar

1 tsp (5 mL) fresh ginger purée

2 tsp (10 mL) crushed toasted sesame
   seeds (see page 80)

¼ tsp (1 mL) cayenne pepper

¼ tsp (1 mL) sweet paprika

Pinch sugar

As with all Asian people, Koreans love street food, so visitors will find no end of fritters, pancakes, steamed custards and soups to satisfy the slightest pangs of hunger. Small crab cakes or squares of rice flour pancakes served with a tangy dipping sauce such as this are especially popular.

These mouthwatering pancakes are known in Korea as "pizzas," but to Western palates they bear little resemblance to the classic Italian version. They are served straight from the sizzling pan in which they are cooked, immediately cut into squares, and dipped into a sauce with chopsticks.

Mix the soy sauce and vinegar together and stir in the other ingredients.

Pajon SCALLION AND SHRIMP PANCAKES

¾ cup (175 mL) all-purpose flour

¾ cup (175 mL) rice flour

Salt and pepper

1 large egg, beaten

1 cup (225 mL) cold water

1 tsp (5 mL) sesame oil

1 tbsp (15 mL) vegetable oil

4 scallions, sliced into thin strips

2 oz (50 g) small peeled shrimp

SERVE WITH

1 quantity Vinegar Dipping Sauce

1 Mix the flours and seasoning together in a bowl. Make a well in the center, add the egg, and stir it into the flours gradually with the cold water to make a smooth batter. Stir in the sesame oil and leave to stand for 30 minutes.

2 Heat the vegetable oil in a small heavy, non-stick skillet, about 6 in (15 cm) in diameter. Pour a quarter of the batter into the skillet along with a quarter of the scallions and shrimp.

3 Cook over medium heat for 3 to 4 minutes until the pancake is set and browned underneath then flip it over and cook for a further 2 to 3 minutes. Remove from the pan to a plate and keep warm. Repeat with the remaining ingredients to make four pancakes.

4 Cut the pancakes into squares and serve hot with the Vinegar Dipping Sauce. **SERVES 4**

VARIATIONS Use fine strips of red or green bell pepper or zucchini instead of scallions.

5 Rubs and glazes

An easy way to flavor meat, fish and seafood before it is chargrilled or barbecued. Both the Chinese and Koreans are famous for their chargrilled dishes and many restaurants have small portable grills at each table so diners can cook their own food to ensure it is done to their liking. A blend of spices, used dry or mixed to a paste with a little oil, is spread over food before it is cooked, in the same way that "blackened" herb and spice mixtures are used in Cajun cuisine. Glazes are more liquid mixes of spices and herbs, sugar, or honey and sauces like soy, hoi sin or sweet chile, which are brushed or spooned over food as it cooks. The high sugar content of glazes means they can burn easily while the food remains undercooked, so some thicker cuts of poultry or meat may need to be partially cooked before they are glazed.

Teriyaki glaze

4 tbsp (50 mL) Japanese soy sauce

4 tbsp (50 mL) mirin

2 tbsp (25 mL) sake

1 tbsp (15 mL) soft brown sugar

Teriyaki is Japanese soy sauce flavored with mirin, sake, and sugar which cooks to a shiny, sweet glaze on fish, chicken, or meat when barbecued, broiled or roasted. Marinate the food in the teriyaki mixture first so that it has a chance to absorb the flavors.

The rich, oily flesh of salmon works well in Japanese recipes because it contrasts perfectly with the tangy, sweet and sour seasonings such as soy and mirin. Marinate the fish fillets in the teriyaki mixture for 30 minutes or longer before cooking.

Stir the ingredients together until the sugar dissolves.

Sake no teriyaki TERIYAKI ROAST SALMON

Four 6-oz (175-g) salmon fillets

1 quantity Teriyaki Glaze

SERVE WITH

Shredded daikon (white radish)

Shredded carrot

Shredded scallions

1 Skin the salmon fillets and place in a shallow dish. Cover with the glaze, turning the fillets so they are well coated. Cover and chill for at least 30 minutes.

2 Lift the salmon from the marinade and barbecue or broil for 2 to 3 minutes each side until done, brushing with any glaze left in the dish during cooking.

3 Serve with a garnish of shredded daikon, carrot and scallions. **SERVES 4**

VARIATIONS Brush the glaze over chicken or beef kebobs or use as a stir-fry sauce for strips of steak.

Rice wine glaze

3 tbsp (45 mL) sake

6 tbsp (75 mL) Japanese soy sauce

2 tbsp (25 mL) mirin

½ tsp (2 mL) fresh ginger purée

"Yakimono" is the word the Japanese use to describe barbecued or broiled food, and this simple sauce is used for brushing over fish fillets before they are barbecued on a portable charcoal-burning hibachi grill.

The fish fillets in Kinome yaki may be barbecued, broiled under a conventional broiler or cooked on the stove in a cast-iron grill pan or large skillet. If opting for the latter, choose a skillet with a heavy base. Oil it lightly, and be sure it is very hot before you add the fish or else the fillets will stick. It is unnecessary to thread the fillets onto skewers if you are cooking them in a grill pan or skillet. Japanese sansho pepper is similar to the highly aromatic reddish-brown Szechwan pepper from China.

Mix all the ingredients together.

Kinome yaki BARBECUED FISH WITH JAPANESE PEPPER SAUCE

Four 7-oz (200-g) sea bass or mackerel
   fillets, skin on

Sansho pepper or ground black pepper

1 quantity Rice Wine Glaze

GARNISH WITH

2 tsp (10 mL) finely chopped scallion
   (green part only)

1 Place the fish fillets on a board, skin-side down, and make several cuts across into the flesh without cutting all the way through the skin. Thread two thin metal skewers side by side through the flesh and down the length of the skin so the fillets can easily be turned on a barbecue. Alternatively, use a special grill for barbecuing fish.

2 Season the fillets with pepper and brush with some of the glaze. Cook flesh-side down first over moderate heat for 3 minutes, then brush on more glaze and cook for another 1 minute until golden brown.

3 Turn the fillets over, brush with more glaze, and cook for 2 minutes more, or until the skin is browned and crisp.

4 Spoon remaining glaze over the fish and serve sprinkled with the scallion.

SERVES 4

VARIATIONS The same glaze can be brushed over brochettes of thin slices of steak or shrimp.

Sake, mirin, and soy glaze

This is used as a glaze for yakitori, the chicken and vegetable kebobs that are cooked on open charcoal grills in Japanese restaurants, their tantalizing aroma attracting plenty of customers.

These yakitori are delicious. Cut the vegetables and chicken into similar-sized pieces so they cook evenly. Any sauce left over after cooking can be spooned over the skewers before serving.

Put the ingredients in a small saucepan and heat until bubbling. Simmer for 5 minutes so the sauce reduces by about one third. Allow to cool.

⅔ cup (150 mL) Japanese soy sauce
½ cup (125 mL) sake
4 tbsp (50 mL) mirin
1 tbsp (15 mL) sugar

Yakitori CHICKEN AND VEGETABLE SKEWERS

1 Thread the chicken pieces, mushrooms, scallions and bell pepper pieces alternately onto bamboo skewers that have previously been soaked in cold water for 30 minutes.
2 Broil the yakitori for 10 minutes, turning the skewers over regularly and brushing with more of the sauce as they cook.
3 Serve with any remaining sauce spooned over the kebobs or in a small bowl as a dip. Accompany with Japanese noodles tossed with a little soy sauce.

SERVES 4

VARIATIONS Yakitori can be made with half chicken and half firm tofu, or all tofu if preferred.

4 chicken breasts, skinned and cut into 1-in (2.5-cm) cubes
8 shiitake mushrooms
6 scallions, trimmed and cut into 1-in (2.5-cm) lengths
1 red bell pepper, seeded and cut into chunks
1 orange bell pepper, seeded and cut into chunks
1 quantity Sake, Mirin, and Soy Glaze

Lime, turmeric, and coconut glaze

Nyonya cuisine began to evolve in the Malay Peninsula in the 15th century when Chinese merchants flocked to the Malay city of Melaka, which had become an important trading center. Some decided to settle there and took Malay wives, the descendants of these unions becoming known as Straits Chinese or Peranakan. Their way of life, language and food are a unique part of the multicultural melting pot that is modern Singapore. Among the essential ingredients in Nyonya cooking are coconut milk, galangal, palm sugar, and lime, all of which are used in this recipe.

The banana leaves used in this recipe should be steamed or blanched for a few minutes until limp before they are used to wrap the shrimp.

Mix together the turmeric, lime juice, garlic, chile, galangal, shallots, shrimp paste, and palm sugar and then stir in the coconut cream until evenly blended.

1 tsp (5 mL) turmeric

Juice of 1 lime

1 clove garlic, peeled and minced

1 red chile, seeded and finely chopped

½-in (1-cm) piece galangal, peeled and finely chopped

2 shallots, finely chopped

½ tsp (2 mL) shrimp paste

2 tsp (10 mL) palm sugar

¼ cup (100 mL) coconut cream

Pais udang SPICY SHRIMP IN BANANA LEAVES

1 Rinse the shrimp and pat dry with paper towels. Season lightly with salt and pepper.
2 Place the banana leaves on a flat surface and divide the shrimp among them. Spoon the glaze over the shrimp and wrap with the banana leaves, securing each parcel with a cocktail or a short satay stick, or string.
3 Broil for about 5 minutes until the shrimp are done. Serve immediately, leaving diners to unwrap the parcels themselves. **SERVES 4**

VARIATIONS Cubes of chicken or a firm white fish such as monkfish can also be used.

1 lb (450 g) medium-sized raw shrimp, peeled

Salt and pepper

8 pieces banana leaves, about 5 in (13 cm) square, steamed or blanched until limp

1 quantity Lime, Turmeric, and Coconut Glaze

EQUIPMENT

Cocktail or short satay sticks, or string

Soy and ginger glaze

2 tbsp (25 mL) rice vinegar

2 tbsp (25 mL) water

¼ cup (50 mL) soft brown sugar

1 tsp (5 mL) fresh ginger purée

6 tbsp (75 mL) Japanese soy sauce

Pumpkin is a popular vegetable in Korea and its bright orange flesh and sweet flavor are particularly suited to this warm soy and ginger glaze.

A selection of salads and vegetable dishes known as panchan, or side dishes, always accompany Korean meals. This pumpkin recipe could also be served with meat, poultry and fish dishes.

Stir the rice vinegar, 2 tablespoons water, and the sugar together until the sugar dissolves. Stir in the ginger and soy sauce.

Yachaejorim SOY AND GINGER GLAZED PUMPKIN

1½ lb (675 g) pumpkin

2 cloves garlic, peeled and minced

2 tbsp (25 mL) vegetable oil

1 quantity Soy and Ginger Glaze

GARNISH WITH

Snipped chives

1 Preheat the oven to 375°F (190°C).

2 Cut the pumpkin into wedges, scoop out the seeds and inner fibres. Peel and chop the flesh into 1½-in (4-cm) chunks. Place in a bowl and mix with the garlic and vegetable oil, then spread out in a roasting pan and roast in the oven for 15 minutes until the pumpkin is almost tender.

3 Spoon the glaze over the pumpkin pieces, turning until coated. Return to the oven for a further 10 minutes or until the pumpkin is tender and well glazed. Garnish with snipped chives.

SERVES 4 AS A VEGETABLE ACCOMPANIMENT

VARIATIONS Butternut squash or sweet potatoes can be cooked in the same way.

Sesame, soy, and ginger glaze

Barbecued meat, particularly beef, is very popular in Korea. On weekends families in Seoul and other cities will get together to eat at one of the numerous outdoor restaurants where each table has its own portable charcoal or gas grill.

For this recipe, the beef can also be cooked in a cast-iron ridged grill pan or heavy skillet, if preferred. In Korea, once the strips of beef have had a chance to marinate in the glaze, diners lift them out with chopsticks and toss them on the charcoal grill to cook. Diners cook their own meat to their taste, then serve it with accompaniments such as shredded carrot and scallions, wedges of crisp Asian pear (nashi) and kimchi pickle (see page 43). Sometimes large leaves of iceberg or other lettuce are served on the side for diners to fill with the meat and vegetables, roll up and dip in soy sauce before eating.

Mix all the ingredients together in a shallow dish until the sugar dissolves.

4 tbsp (50 mL) Japanese soy sauce

2 cloves garlic, peeled and minced

3 scallions, finely chopped

1-in (2.5-cm) piece gingerroot, peeled and grated

1 tsp (5 mL) sesame oil

1 tbsp (15 mL) soft brown sugar

1 tbsp (15 mL) sesame seeds

Bulgogi BARBECUED BEEF

1 Add the steak to the glaze in a shallow dish and turn until coated. Set aside to marinate for 1 hour or longer.
2 Have ready the pickle, shredded carrots and scallions, pear wedges, and lettuce leaves before you start cooking.
3 Heat a cast-iron grill pan until very hot. Using chopsticks or tongs, lift the beef slices onto the pan a few at a time, and cook until done to your liking, turning them over occasionally. They should be sticky and caramelized on the outside and tender inside.
4 Fill the lettuce leaves with the beef, pickle, carrots, scallions, and pear wedges. Roll up, and serve with soy sauce for dipping. **SERVES 4**

VARIATIONS Although traditionally made with beef, this recipe is also made with pork or lamb.

1 lb 2 oz (500 g) fillet or sirloin steak, cut into thin slices

1 quantity Sesame, Soy, and Ginger Glaze

SERVE WITH

Large lettuce leaves

Kimchi pickle

Shredded carrots and scallions

Asian pear (nashi) wedges

Soy sauce for dipping

1 tbsp (15 mL) sesame oil

4 tbsp (50 mL) dark soy sauce

4 cloves garlic, peeled and minced

2 tsp (10 mL) fresh ginger purée

1 tsp (5 mL) chili powder

2 tsp (5 mL) sugar

Ground black pepper to taste

2 lb (900 g) pork spareribs, cut into
    four servings

1 quantity Soy and Chili Barbecue Glaze

2 tbsp (25 mL) sesame seeds, lightly
    toasted

GARNISH WITH

Fresh cilantro leaves, sliced radishes,
    shredded cabbage, or lettuce sprigs

Soy and chili barbecue glaze

Sesame, garlic, chili, and ginger are four of the basic flavorings of Korean cuisine and here they are combined to make an aromatic glaze for barbecued meat. Try to track down Korean chili powder to make the glaze authentic. Quite coarsely ground, it has a fairly mild flavor—somewhere between sweet paprika and cayenne pepper—and is vivid scarlet in color, giving Korean dishes their characteristically vibrant hue. If Korean chili powder is not available, Mexican chili powder may be used.

The traditional accompaniment to Kalbigui is kimchi (see page 43), a spicy Korean dish of shredded cabbage that is served at almost every meal. To toast sesame seeds, spread white sesame seeds over the base of a heavy dry skillet and place over moderate heat. Leave until the seeds start to color, turning regularly. As soon as they are golden, remove from the pan and allow to cool. If you cool them in the pan they will scorch and burn before the pan is cold.

Mix all the ingredients together until evenly combined and you have a smooth, paste-like consistency.

Kalbigui GLAZED CHARGRILLED SPARERIBS

1 Place the spareribs in a dish. Cover with the glaze, turning several times until thoroughly coated. Leave in a cool place to marinate for at least 4 hours.

2 Preheat the broiler or barbecue. Lift the spareribs from the dish and broil or barbecue for about 10 minutes on each side until done, brushing with any marinade remaining in the dish.

3 Serve hot, sprinkled with sesame seeds. Garnish with sprigs of fresh cilantro, sliced radishes, and shredded cabbage or lettuce sprigs. **SERVES 4**

VARIATIONS This glaze could be used for pork chops or chicken thighs. For these, the cooking time needs to be increased to around 15 to 20 minutes, depending on the thickness of the meat.

Honey, sweet soy, and lime glaze

3 tbsp (45 mL) clear honey

2 tbsp (25 mL) sweet soy sauce

1 tbsp (15 mL) lime juice

1 tsp (5 mL) annatto seed oil or 1 tsp
(5 mL) paprika and ½ tsp (2 mL)
turmeric mixed with 2 tsp (10 mL)
peanut oil

Annatto are small red seeds from the "lipstick plant." The seeds are fried in oil to extract their color, and this oil is strained to provide the orange oil used to color and flavor Asian dishes. The oil can be bought from Oriental grocery stores but if it is not available, paprika and turmeric mixed with oil, rather than fried in it, can be substituted.

This recipe shows a sophisticated Vietnamese method of roasting chicken for a special occasion. The chicken is first marinated in a seasoned sesame mixture that is spooned into the cavity. It is then coated with a sticky honey glaze and roasted, with more of the sesame marinade basted over it from time to time as it cooks. Carve the chicken into joints for serving. The traditional Vietnamese accompaniment would be glutinous rice.

Mix the ingredients together in a bowl.

Ga quay mat ong

CHICKEN ROASTED WITH A HONEY, LEMON, AND GARLIC GLAZE

3½-lb (1.6-kg) chicken

2 tsp (10 mL) freshly ground black pepper

1 tsp (5 mL) salt

2 tbsp (25 mL) sugar

2 tsp (10 mL) sesame oil

2 tbsp (25 mL) peanut oil

1 quantity Honey, Sweet Soy, and
Lime Glaze

1 Rinse the chicken inside and out and pat dry with paper towels. Mix the black pepper, salt, sugar, and sesame oil together and spoon inside the chicken, turning the bird over so the inside is evenly coated. Truss the bird with thin twine or close the body cavity with a skewer. Set aside in a cool place for 1 hour.

2 Preheat the oven to 375°F (190°C). Place the chicken in a roasting pan, drizzle the peanut oil over it and roast for 30 minutes. Brush half the glaze over the chicken. Roast for a further 30 minutes, and baste and brush with the remaining glaze. Roast for a final 30 minutes, basting every 10 minutes until the chicken juices run clear when the thickest part of the leg is pierced with a skewer.

3 Serve with glutinous rice. **SERVES 4**

VARIATIONS Turkey or duck may be roasted in the same way.

6 Stews and braised dishes

The Western style of slowly braising meat or poultry in a sauce redolent with tomatoes, bell peppers and olives is just one of the Mediterranean legacies bequeathed to Filipino cooks when their country was a Spanish colony. Other countries in Southeast Asia "braise" food as well but, in keeping with their more traditional cooking methods, their braising is a far quicker process and generally involves frying the fish, bean curd, meat or seafood first and then simmering it for just a few minutes in a flavorful sauce based on soy, tamarind, rice wine or sesame. Bo kho, the spicy, slow-cooked beef stew of Vietnam, is one exception to the "Asian brief braise" rule. Like the Filipinos, Vietnamese cooks have also been influenced by Western cuisine, in their case French, the legacy of the long years of French rule in Indochina.

Beer and garlic braising sauce

Another legacy of French rule in Vietnam is to add beer to the cooking liquid of a stew or braise in order to tenderize the meat and flavor the sauce.

A good-quality braising steak or a lean roasting cut works best in this stew. Trim any fat from the meat, cut it into even-sized pieces, and brown in the oil in batches. Too many pieces added to the browning pan at once will lower the heat and prevent the meat from sealing quickly and remaining tender when done.

3 cloves garlic, peeled and minced

1 tbsp (15 mL) curry paste

2 tbsp (25 mL) fish sauce

1 tsp (5 mL) sugar

1¼ cups (300 mL) beer

Mix all the ingredients together.

Bo kho SPICY BEEF STEW

1½ lb (675 g) braising steak, cut into
   1½-in (4-cm) cubes

2 tbsp (25 mL) peanut oil

1 large onion, peeled and finely chopped

2 carrots, peeled and sliced

1 quantity Beer and Garlic Braising Sauce

1¼ cups (300 mL) beef stock (1 CAN)

8-fl oz (225-mL) can plum tomatoes

2 star anise

Salt and pepper

1 Preheat the oven to 325°F (170°C).

2 Brown the beef in batches in the oil in a thick-bottomed casserole over brisk heat, removing each batch as it browns before adding the next.

3 When all the meat has been browned, remove it from the casserole, lower the heat and add the onion and carrots. Fry gently for 5 minutes, then add the braising sauce, stock, tomatoes, and star anise. Bring to a boil, lower the heat, and return the beef to the casserole.

4 Season, cover, and cook in the oven for 1¼ hours or until the beef and carrots are tender. Remove the star anise and serve at once or reheat when needed. Accompany with boiled or roasted sweet potatoes. **SERVES 4**

VARIATION Use lean pork and reduce the time in the oven by about 30 minutes.

PRESSURE COOK – 45 MIN. 40

Chile and tomato sauce

1 tbsp (15 mL) chile sauce

2 tbsp (25 mL) light soy sauce

1 tbsp (15 mL) sugar

2 tbsp (25 mL) vinegar

4 tbsp (50 mL) tomato ketchup

1 tsp (5 mL) sesame oil

Crab braised in a tomato and chile sauce, served with noodles or sometimes French bread to mop up the sauce, is one of Singapore's favorite dishes and there is no finer place to enjoy it than in one of the open-fronted restaurants at the UDMC Seafood Center on the East Coast Parkway, which runs from Changhi Airport into the city. Every night the tables are packed as customers come not just for chile crab but for steamed shrimp, mee goreng fried noodles, pepper crab, crisp baby squid in a sweet soy sauce, and many other gastronomic delights.

For this recipe you will need to buy freshly cooked crab claws or whole crabs cut into pieces. The rempah spice paste is fried before the crab and sauce are added and the beaten egg helps thicken and enrich the sauce. The dish is eaten with the fingers, so provide guests with finger bowls of warm water (or tea, as would be offered in Singapore).

Mix all the ingredients together in a bowl.

Chile Crab

REMPAH

1-in (2.5-cm) piece gingerroot, peeled and sliced

2 cloves garlic, peeled and chopped

4 shallots, peeled and chopped

4 tbsp (50 mL) vegetable oil

OTHER INGREDIENTS

2¼ lb (1.2 kg) freshly cooked crabs, cleaned and cut into pieces

1 quantity Chile and Tomato Sauce

1 cup (225 mL) chicken stock

1 tbsp (15 mL) cornstarch blended with 3 tbsp (45 mL) water

1 egg, beaten

1 To make the rempah, grind the gingerroot, garlic, and shallots together to make a paste, or pound them with a mortar and pestle. Heat half the oil in a small saucepan, add the rempah, and fry over medium heat until fragrant, about 5 minutes.

2 Heat the remaining oil in a wok and stir-fry the crab over high heat for 2 minutes. Add the fried rempah and the sauce, mixing thoroughly so the crab is coated. Pour in the stock and bring to a boil. Simmer for 10 minutes, then add the cornstarch mixture. Boil until thickened. Stir in the egg and mix well.

3 Transfer the crab pieces to a serving plate and serve immediately. Accompany with noodles covered with the sauce or with French bread to mop up the sauce. **SERVES 4**

VARIATIONS Prepare with uncooked jumbo shrimp or scallops instead of crab.

Red braising sauce

"Red-cooked" is a popular way to serve whole fish in China. Freshwater carp would be the most commonly used fish but porgy, sea bass, or red snapper could also be used. The whole fish are broiled or fried first, then braised in this sweet-sour sauce.

This recipe works best using one fish such as a red snapper large enough to serve four people, or four smaller fish such as porgy, mullet, carp, or even trout. Clean and descale the fish and slash the skin on each side several times before cooking.

1 tsp (5 mL) fresh ginger purée
1 tbsp (15 mL) light soy sauce
1 tbsp (15 mL) rice wine or dry sherry
1 tsp (5 mL) sweet chile sauce
3 tbsp (45 mL) yellow bean sauce
¼ cup (100 mL) fish stock
1 tsp (5 mL) sugar

Mix all the ingredients together.

Hung siu fish RED-COOKED FISH

1 Wash the fish inside and out and pat dry with paper towels. With a small sharp knife, make several cuts through the skin on each side of the fish.
2 Heat the oil in a wok, add the fish, and cook for 3 to 4 minutes, turning over once. Do this in batches if it is difficult to comfortably fry all the fish in the wok together.
3 Remove the fish and sprinkle them with the sesame oil. Add the sauce to the wok, bring to a simmer, and return the fish to the wok. Baste the fish with the sauce and braise gently for 5 minutes, turning them over once.
4 Serve the fish with the sauce spooned over it, garnished with shredded scallions, carrot, bamboo shoots, and Chinese chives. **SERVES 4**

1 large or 4 small fish, e.g., snapper, carp,
  or mullet, cleaned and descaled
2 tbsp (25 mL) peanut oil
Few drops sesame oil
1 quantity Red Braising Sauce

GARNISH WITH

Shredded scallions
Shredded carrot
Shredded bamboo shoots
Chinese chives

VARIATION Use thick white fish fillets instead of whole fish.

Chile bean, soy, and ginger sauce

Unlike other Chinese bean sauces, toban jiang (chile bean paste) is made with broad beans rather than soy beans. The broad beans grow in the fertile Chengdu Plains of Szechwan province and are made into a paste with red chiles, flour, and seasonings through a process that involves two fermentations in large earthenware jars separated by nearly two months of drying in the sun.

When making the Szechwan shrimp recipe below, cook the shrimp first in the wok then remove before making the sauce. The shrimp can be cooked whole or with their heads removed. But leave their shells on so the delicate flesh is protected from the hot oil. As the shrimp are eaten with the fingers, provide a small finger bowl of warm water with a slice of lemon for each diner.

Heat the oil in a wok, add the chile bean paste, ginger purée, and garlic and cook gently for 2 minutes, stirring frequently. Stir in the other ingredients.

1 tbsp (15 mL) peanut oil
1 tbsp (15 mL) toban jiang (Szechwan chile bean paste)
1 tsp (5 mL) fresh ginger purée
2 cloves garlic, peeled and minced
1 tbsp (15 mL) rice vinegar
2 tbsp (25 mL) light soy sauce
1 tsp (5 mL) light brown sugar
2/3 cup (150 mL) fish stock

Sichuan loong haw SZECHWAN-STYLE BRAISED SHRIMP

1 Remove the heads from the shrimp or leave on, as preferred. With a small pair of sharp scissors, cut each shrimp down its back through the shell and pull out the black "vein" running down it, leaving the shell in place.
2 Heat the oil in a wok and stir-fry the shrimp in two batches for 5 minutes or until they turn pink.
3 Remove the shrimp from the wok. Make the sauce as directed above and boil rapidly for 2 minutes. Return the shrimp to the wok and toss for 2 to 3 minutes until heated through and most of the liquid in the pan has evaporated.
4 Serve at once with shredded scallions. **SERVES 4**

VARIATIONS This dish works well with a mixture of seafood such as squid, mussels and queen scallops, as well as shrimp.

20 jumbo shrimp
2 tbsp (25 mL) peanut oil
1 quantity Chile Bean, Soy, and Ginger Sauce

GARNISH WITH

Shredded scallions

Sake and sweet soy sauce

¾ cup (200 mL) Japanese soy sauce

½ cup (150 mL) sake

½ cup (150 mL) water

½ cup (125 mL) sugar

A sweet-savory sauce served with beef and vegetables to make one of Japan's most famous dishes, sukiyaki. It became popular in Japan at the beginning of the last century when the Japanese began eating beef which had previously been forbidden under Buddhist laws. Two styles of sukiyaki exist: in Osaka the sauce is cooked at the table as different ingredients are added, and in Tokyo the sauce is prepared in advance as in this recipe.

A close relative of the Mongolian fire pot, hot pot and steamboat dishes—where raw ingredients are dropped into a central pot of steaming broth—crop up all over Southeast Asia, particularly around the Mekong Delta. The Thais also have their own version of steamboat, calling it suki, which is short for Japan's sukiyaki. Although special sukiyaki pans may be bought from Japanese stores, an electric frying pan or a heavy frying pan on a portable table works well. Shirataki are translucent jelly-like threads made from a root vegetable similar to yam and are available fresh in packages. Rice vermicelli, soaked in hot water until soft, could be substituted. In Japan, a green leafy vegetable called shungiku (similar to Chinese chrysanthemum leaves) would be used for the recipe. Since both are difficult to obtain, except from Oriental grocers, baby spinach leaves are used here.

Put all the ingredients in a saucepan and bring slowly to a boil, stirring occasionally so the sugar dissolves.

Sukiyaki BEEF AND VEGETABLE HOT POT WITH SWEET SOY SAUCE

1 lb (450 g) sirloin steak

12 shiitake mushrooms

8 oz (225 g) fresh shirataki, drained, rinsed and cut into 6-in (15-cm) lengths

4 scallions, sliced

4½ oz (125 g) baby spinach leaves, rinsed and sliced

7 oz (200 g) firm tofu, cubed

4 small eggs

1 quantity Sake and Sweet Soy Sauce

1 Trim the fat from the steak and keep to one side for greasing the pan. Slice the steak very thinly. Cut a small cross in the top of each mushroom.

2 Arrange the steak, shirataki, scallions, mushrooms, baby spinach leaves, and tofu on individual serving platters. Break the eggs into individual dipping bowls and beat lightly. Pour the sauce into a jug.

3 Heat the Sukiyaki pan, add the beef fat, and cook gently until just enough fat is rendered to grease the base of the pan. Remove the remaining fat and discard.

4 Add one quarter of the beef and stir-fry for 1 to 2 minutes. Add a quarter of the vegetables, tofu, shirataki, and sauce and simmer until the ingredients are cooked.

5 Diners pick ingredients out of the pan with chopsticks as they wish, dipping each ingredient into the beaten egg before eating. Add the remaining ingredients and sauce to the pan in batches as needed. **SERVES 4**

VARIATIONS Any combination of dipping ingredients, such as shredded bok choy, wedges of white or red onion, and sliced bamboo shoots.

Lime and lemongrass sauce

An aromatic paste of fresh herbs and spices to which thick coconut milk is added to make a braising sauce for chicken. Tamarind is often included to provide a sour tang to balance the creaminess of the coconut, but in this recipe lime juice is used instead.

This fresh chicken dish can be made ahead and left in a cool place for several hours so the chicken has time to absorb all the flavors of the sauce. When ready to serve, only reheat the dish until the chicken is hot all the way through or it will overcook and become tough.

1 Place the onions, chiles, garlic, lemongrass, and ginger or galangal in a food processor with half the oil, and blend to a paste. Mix in the turmeric.
2 Heat the remaining oil in a saucepan, add the paste, and fry for 6 to 7 minutes over medium heat until cooked through and aromatic. Gradually stir in the coconut milk and then the lime juice.

2 red onions, peeled and chopped
2 red chiles, seeded and chopped
2 cloves garlic, peeled and sliced
1 stalk lemongrass, chopped
1-in (2.5-cm) piece gingerroot or galangal, peeled and chopped
2 tbsp (25 mL) peanut oil
1 tsp (5 mL) ground turmeric
1 cup (250 mL) thick coconut milk
Juice of 1 lime

Ayam limau purut CHICKEN IN LIME AND LEMONGRASS SAUCE

1 Put the sauce in a saucepan and stir in the chicken stock. Heat until gently bubbling, then add the chicken and lime leaves. Simmer uncovered for 20 to 25 minutes or until the chicken is done.
2 Season to taste and serve with rice or egg noodles. **SERVES 4**

VARIATION Raw peeled medium-sized or large shrimp can also be cooked in the sauce but will only need to be simmered 5 to 8 minutes until the shrimp turn pink.

1 quantity Lime and Lemongrass Sauce
⅔ cup (150 mL) chicken stock
8 chicken thighs, skinned, or 4 chicken breasts, skinned and each cut into 3 or 4 pieces
2 kaffir lime leaves, cut into wafer-thin slices
Salt and pepper

Three-flavor sauce

2 tbsp (25 mL) peanut oil

2 cloves garlic, peeled and minced

1 tsp (5 mL) fresh ginger purée

1 medium red chile, seeded and chopped

2 shallots, peeled and finely chopped

2 tbsp (25 mL) palm sugar or soft
    brown sugar

1 tsp (5 mL) tamarind paste

1 tbsp (15 mL) nam pla (Thai fish sauce)

Juice of 3 limes

This sauce crops up all over Thailand in many different guises and is a balance of sour, sweet, and salty flavors. Although it contains a little chile, it is not hot but additional chiles can be added to taste.

Lovers of hot food can add extra fire by serving this chicken dish with nam prik (chile sauce) as a condiment, if other diners prefer not to have the chile content increased in the Three-Flavor Sauce. Bok choy or snow peas, either steamed or stir-fried, make a good accompaniment.

Heat the oil in a wok and fry the garlic, ginger, chile, and shallots over a low heat for 3 minutes. Crumble in the sugar and cook until it caramelizes to a rich, red brown. Add the tamarind paste, fish sauce, and lime juice and remove from the heat.

Gai tod saparot

CHICKEN AND PINEAPPLE WITH THREE-FLAVOR SAUCE

2 tbsp (25 mL) peanut oil

6 boneless chicken thighs, skinned and
    cut into bite-sized pieces

4 scallions, trimmed and sliced

1 slice pineapple, cut into small pieces

1 quantity Three-Flavor Sauce

⅔ cup (150 mL) chicken stock

4 kaffir lime leaves, cut into wafer
    thin strips

1 Heat the oil in a skillet and stir-fry the chicken in two batches for 1 to 2 minutes over brisk heat. Remove and set aside.
2 Add the scallions and pineapple to the skillet and stir-fry for 1 minute. Transfer the scallions and pineapple to the Three-Flavor Sauce in the wok, stir in the stock, and bring to a simmer.
3 Lower the heat, add the chicken and lime leaves, and cook gently for 10 minutes.
4 Serve with a green vegetable such as bok choy or snow peas and rice or noodles. **SERVES 4**

VARIATION Replace the chicken with raw shrimp.

Rich tomato sauce

From 1521 until 1898 the Spanish ruled the Philippines, naming the country after King Philip II of Spain and also bringing a touch of the Mediterranean to its cuisine. Paella, gambas picantes, leche flan, and pochero are all Spanish dishes that turn up on Filipino tables on festive occasions with tomatoes, saffron, chorizo sausages and olives featuring alongside more traditional local fare.

Despite Spain's influence over Filipino cuisine, Pochero actually owes more to a French pot au feu. The meat and vegetables are usually eaten first and then the cooking sauce is served separately as a soup. To serve, ladle the stew into deep bowls and provide a soup spoon alongside each person's knife and fork.

1 Heat the oil in a pan, add the onion, and cook over low heat until softened.
2 Add the red bell pepper and garlic and cook for a further 5 minutes, stirring occasionally.
3 Add the tomatoes, tomato paste, stock, and seasoning and bring to a boil. Lower the heat and simmer for 10 minutes.

2 tbsp (25 mL) vegetable oil
1 large onion, peeled and sliced
1 red bell pepper, seeded and sliced
3 cloves garlic, peeled and minced
Two 14-fl oz (398-mL) cans chopped
   tomatoes
2 tbsp (25 mL) tomato paste
1¼ cups (300 mL) chicken stock
Salt and pepper

Pochero MIXED MEAT AND VEGETABLE STEW

1 Heat the oil in a flameproof (thick-bottomed) casserole and fry the pork in batches until lightly browned. Remove from the casserole and set aside. Add the chicken and chorizo sausages and fry for 3 minutes until the chicken is pale and starting to brown a little at the edges.
2 Add the tomato sauce, chickpeas and potatoes and return the pork to the casserole. Bring to simmering point, cover with a lid, and cook gently for 30 minutes.
3 Uncover the pan and cook for a further 10 minutes or until the liquid has reduced and thickened a little. Adjust the seasoning and serve in deep soup plates. **SERVES 4**

2 tbsp (25 mL) vegetable oil
12 oz (350 g) pork steaks, cut into
   small pieces
2 chicken breasts, cut into small pieces
2 chorizo sausages, cut into chunks
1 quantity Rich Tomato Sauce
14-fl oz (398-mL) can chickpeas, drained
   and rinsed
1 lb (450 g) potatoes, peeled and cut into
   small chunks

VARIATIONS Use canned kidney, fava, or cannellini beans instead of chickpeas.

Onion, chile, and tomato sauce

2 tbsp (25 mL) olive oil

2 large onions, peeled and thinly sliced

1 red chile, seeded and finely chopped

3 cloves garlic, peeled and minced

1 tsp (5 mL) ground cinnamon

1 tbsp (15 mL) vinegar

2 tsp (10 mL) cornstarch

2 cups (450 mL) lamb stock

2 tbsp (25 mL) tomato paste

1 tsp (5 mL) ground black pepper

Just as Serani (Eurasian) dishes in Malaysia have been influenced by the cooking and cultures of other nations, so China, Spain, the Malay Peninsula, and America have all had a hand in developing the Filipino cuisine of today. Stews and casseroles are popular throughout the islands. Bundles of seasoning herbs and spices known as ricado (usually bay leaves, peppercorns, and cinnamon sticks) are sold as local "bouquets garnis."

In the Philippines, Caldareta would probably be made with goat meat which would first be marinated in vinegar to help tenderize it. The stew can be cooked on the stove over a low heat or in the oven until the lamb and vegetables are tender. Choose "waxy" potatoes (new potatoes, for example) that are firm rather than "floury" when cooked.

1 Heat the oil in a saucepan, add the onions, and cook over gentle heat until softened. Add the chile and garlic and cook for a further 5 minutes until the onions are golden.

2 Add the cinnamon, stir well, then add the vinegar. Mix the cornstarch with a little of the lamb stock and stir into the casserole with the remaining stock and the tomato paste. Bring to a boil, then lower the heat and season with the pepper.

Caldareta LAMB STEW WITH POTATOES AND PEPPERS

2 tbsp (25 mL) olive oil

1½ lb (675 g) lean lamb steaks, cut into cubes

1 lb (450 g) potatoes, peeled and cut into medium-sized pieces

2 carrots, cut into chunks

1 quantity Onion, Chile, and Tomato Sauce

2 bay leaves

1 red bell pepper, seeded and cut into chunks

12 pitted green olives

1 Heat the oil in a flameproof (thick-bottomed) casserole and brown the lamb in batches over brisk heat, removing one batch of meat before adding the next.

2 When all the meat has been browned, return the meat to the casserole with the potatoes and carrots and add the sauce and bay leaves.
Bring to a boil, cover, and simmer gently on the stove for 1 hour or cook in the oven at 350°F (180°C) for the same time.

3 Add the bell pepper to the casserole and cook for a further 20 minutes. Remove the bay leaves and stir in the olives just before serving. **SERVES 4**

VARIATION Use cubed pork shoulder instead of lamb and reduce the initial cooking time from 1 hour to 45 minutes.

7 Curries

Although usually associated with the cuisines of India and Sri Lanka, curries are popular all over Southeast Asia. "Kari" derives from the southern Indian Tamil word for sauce. The custom of blending aromatic spice mixes to flavor the cooking liquid of a dish gained popularity as plantation workers and traders moved around the region, incorporating local ingredients and cooking techniques into their own cuisines as they went. Chinese curries are mild and aromatic, Thai curries are fiery with chiles, and curries from Myanmar (Burma), Laos and the Mekong Delta balance the fresh citrus flavors of lemongrass and lime with the pungency of fish sauce. Coconut milk or ground nuts are used to thicken and enrich sauces, with accompaniments ranging from steamed rice and glass noodles to sour pickled vegetables and chile-packed sambals.

Red curry paste

A classic Indonesian spice paste used for making slow-cooked curries. Red chiles are indigenous to the native cuisine and are either added fresh as in this curry paste or as sambal oelek, a highly piquant sauce made from minced chiles (and their seeds) and vinegar. Kencur is a highly aromatic rhizome similar to ginger and should be used sparingly.

Long, slow cooking means the beef in this dish becomes deliciously tender and full of flavor as it absorbs the spices and coconut milk. Quite dry, this is a popular dish in Padang, western Sumatra, where it would traditionally be served with sticky rice cooked in coconut milk or even packed into bread to make a sandwich. Although rendang is usually made with beef, buffalo is a popular alternative in Sumatra.

2 red onions, peeled and chopped

4 cloves garlic, peeled and chopped

6 medium red chiles, seeded and chopped

1 tsp (5 mL) ground kencur or 1-in (2.5-cm) piece gingerroot, peeled and finely chopped

⅔ cup (150 mL) coconut milk

Blend all the ingredients together to a thick paste in a food processor.

Rendang sapi INDONESIAN RED BEEF CURRY

3 tbsp (45 mL) vegetable oil

1 quantity Red Curry Paste

1 lb 9 oz (700 g) rump steak, cubed

1 tsp (5 mL) turmeric

1 tbsp (15 mL) ground coriander

6 curry leaves

⅔ cup (150 mL) coconut milk

1 tbsp (15 mL) tamarind pulp, infused in ⅔ cup (150 mL) boiling water for 10 minutes, then strained

2 tsp (10 mL) palm sugar or soft brown sugar

Salt

1 Heat the oil in a large heavy saucepan, add the curry paste, and cook over low heat for 5 minutes.

2 Add the steak, turmeric, ground coriander, and curry leaves, stir well and cook gently for a further 10 minutes.

3 Stir in the coconut milk and strained tamarind liquid and cook, covered, over the lowest possible heat for 1 hour then uncover and cook for a further 30 minutes until the meat is tender and the sauce has reduced and thickened.

4 Stir in the sugar and add salt to season, if necessary. Serve with rice.

SERVES 4

VARIATIONS This recipe can be made using a lean cut of lamb such as leg. Chicken may also be used but the cooking time will need to be reduced.

Chinese curry powder

1-in (2.5-cm) piece gingerroot, peeled and
  chopped
1-in (2.5-cm) piece cinnamon stick
2 tbsp (25 mL) coriander seeds
1 tsp (5 mL) Szechwan black peppercorns
1 tsp (5 mL) fennel seeds
1 tbsp (15 mL) ground turmeric

Curries became part of the cuisines of southern and eastern China when emigrants returned home from the Malay Peninsula and India and brought their adopted countries' spicy powders and pastes with them. Chinese curries tend to be more aromatic and less fiery than Thai or southern Indian curries as chile is not included in the spice mix at the beginning but added as an optional extra to the sauce. As well as using the spice blend for curries, Chinese cooks often also add it to marinades or barbecue glazes.

For this recipe it is important to fry the curry powder in the oil over gentle heat for several minutes before the other ingredients are added so that the spices in the finished dish are mellow and aromatic. Serve the curry with boiled rice.

Place the ginger, cinnamon, coriander, peppercorns, and fennel seeds in a spice grinder or mortar and pestle and pound to a powder. Stir in the turmeric.

Ga lei gei CURRIED CHICKEN WITH POTATOES

2 tbsp (25 mL) vegetable oil
1 quantity Chinese Curry Powder
3 medium-sized potatoes, peeled and
  cut into ¾-in (2-cm) cubes
1 large onion, cut into wedges and layers
  separated
1 lb 2 oz (500 g) chicken thighs, skinned
  and cut into bite-sized pieces
1 tsp (5 mL) chile (hot pepper) sauce
  (optional)
1 tbsp (15 mL) dark soy sauce
2 tsp (10 mL) cornstarch
1¾ cups (300 mL) chicken stock

1 Heat the oil in a large skillet, add the curry powder, and fry over gentle heat for 2 minutes.
2 Add the potatoes and onion and cook for 5 minutes. stirring occasionally. Add the chicken, chile sauce, and soy sauce. Stir the cornstarch into a little of the stock and stir into the pan with the remaining stock. Bring to a boil, stirring constantly, then lower the heat, cover the pan, and simmer for 25 minutes or until the potatoes are tender. SERVES 4

VARIATIONS Use lean tender steak such as rump or sirloin instead of chicken. Slice the steak thinly, brown it quickly in the oil and then remove before frying the curry paste. Return it to the pan when the potatoes are almost tender.

Onion, garlic, and ginger curry paste

All Burmese curries are based on onion, garlic, and ginger, which are ground together as a basic paste before chili and turmeric are mixed in. A Burmese curry does not have to be hot and a small amount of chili powder is often used in combination with less pungent spices in order to bring out the flavor of a dish. Sesame is also used in curries with light sesame oil used for frying or a few drops of stronger, Chinese-style sesame oil mixed with peanut or vegetable oil.

Wetha hin is a "wet" curry with an aromatically spicy sauce, rather than a see byan, or "dry" curry, where the stock or water in the saucepan evaporates completely, leaving only the original frying oil. Traditional accompaniments for a Burmese curry are boiled long-grain rice or noodles.

Put the onion, garlic, ginger, and half the oil in a food processor and blend to a paste, stopping the machine regularly to push down the contents of the bowl as they spread up the sides. Heat the remaining oil in a pan, add the paste, and fry over low heat for 5 minutes, stirring frequently, until golden. Add the chili powder and turmeric and fry for a further 2 minutes.

1 large onion, peeled and chopped

4 cloves garlic, peeled and chopped

1-in (2.5-cm) piece gingerroot, peeled and chopped

2 tbsp (25 mL) peanut oil

½ tsp (2 mL) chili powder

1 tsp (5 mL) turmeric

Wetha hin CURRIED PORK IN A SAUCE

1 Heat the peanut and sesame oils in a large, heavy skillet and fry the shallots and pork for 5 minutes over fairly brisk heat, stirring constantly until starting to brown.

2 Lower the heat and stir in the curry paste, brown sugar, ground coriander, shrimp paste, and lemongrass. Fry gently for 2 minutes.

3 Add the chicken stock and coconut milk and bring to a boil. Lower the heat, cover the skillet, and cook gently for 30 minutes, stirring occasionally. Cook the cellophane noodles according to the package instructions and divide into four portions. Ladle the curry over the noodles and serve garnished with the scallions and fresh cilantro. **SERVES 4**

VARIATION Chicken can be used instead of pork in this curry.

2 tbsp (25 mL) peanut oil

Few drops sesame oil

4 shallots, peeled and sliced

1 lb 2 oz (500 g) pork steaks, cut into 1-in (2.5-cm) cubes

1 quantity Onion, Garlic, and Ginger Curry Paste

½ tsp (2 mL) soft brown sugar

1 tbsp (15 mL) ground coriander

1 tsp (5 mL) ngapi (dried shrimp paste)

1 tsp (5 mL) fresh lemongrass purée

1¼ cups (300mL) chicken stock

1¼ cups (300 mL) coconut milk

SERVE WITH

12 oz (350 g) cellophane noodles

4 scallions, sliced

2 tbsp (25 mL) roughly chopped fresh cilantro leaves

Green curry paste

Thai cuisine has a reputation for being fiery and the country's curry dishes are no exception. Chiles are the culprit so the "heat" of the finished dish will depend on the type of chiles used and whether you add their seeds or discard them. As a rule of thumb, the smaller the chile, the hotter it is.

Chicken thighs are ideal for curries as they are more economic than chicken breasts and dry out less when simmered in the sauce. Serve the curry with steamed Thai fragrant rice.Curries in Thailand are colour coded into green, red and yellow-the difference being the colour of the chiles used to make the basic curry paste. Green curries are made from fresh green chiles ground with fresh cilantro, red curries from dried, de-seeded red chiles and yellow from fresh yellow chiles given a boost with ground turmeric. When the word "gaeng" is included in the curry's title it means the sauce is based on a creamy coconut broth.

1 Put all the ingredients in a food processor and blend to a paste. Alternatively, pound the ingredients in a mortar and pestle.
2 Store the paste in a sealed container in the refrigerator and use as needed. It will keep for up to 3 weeks.

6 medium green chiles, seeded and
   coarsely chopped
2 stalks lemongrass, outer leaves removed,
   and chopped
Small bunch fresh cilantro, stalks removed
Small bunch Thai basil, stalks removed
1 shallot, peeled and chopped
1 tsp (5 mL) coriander seeds
1 tsp (5 mL) cumin seeds
2 large cloves garlic, peeled and
   coarsely chopped
1 tsp (5 mL) shrimp paste
1-in (2.5-cm) piece fresh galangal,
   peeled and chopped or 2 tsp
   (10 mL) galangal purée
4 kaffir lime leaves, chopped

Gaeng kheow wan gai THAI GREEN CHICKEN CURRY

1 Heat the oil in a large saucepan, add the shallots and sweet potato, and fry over gentle heat for 5 minutes, stirring occasionally. Add the zucchini and curry paste and fry for a further 2 minutes.
2 Add the chicken, stirring so it is evenly coated in the spice paste, and fry for 5 minutes.
3 Stir in the fish sauce, sugar, and coconut milk and bring to a boil. Lower the heat and simmer gently for 15 minutes until the chicken and sweet potato are done and the sauce has reduced and thickened a little.
4 Serve at once, garnished with the shredded lime leaves and chile. **SERVES 4**

VARIATION A selection of firm white fish and shellfish such as raw shrimp or squid can be substituted for the chicken. Add the fish and shellfish only about 5 minutes before the curry is cooked, so the shrimp do not become tasteless and tough. Avoid stirring the curry too frequently once white fish has been added or its delicate flesh will break and disintegrate.

2 tbsp (25 mL) peanut oil
2 shallots, peeled and sliced
1 sweet potato, peeled and cut into
   small pieces
1 zucchini, trimmed and sliced
2 tbsp (25 mL) Thai Green Curry Paste
1 lb 2 oz (500 g) boneless chicken thighs,
   skinned and cut into chunks
1 tbsp (15 mL) nam pla (Thai fish sauce)
2 tbsp (25 mL) palm sugar or soft
   brown sugar
1½ cups (400 mL) coconut milk
Salt and pepper

GARNISH WITH

3 kaffir lime leaves, shredded
1 red chile, seeded and finely sliced

3 cloves garlic, peeled and chopped

1 large onion, peeled and chopped

1 stalk lemongrass, outer leaves removed
  and stem chopped

1-in (2.5-cm) piece gingerroot, peeled and
  chopped

2 tsp (10 mL) coriander seeds

1 red chile, seeded and chopped

½ tsp (2 mL) turmeric

2 tbsp (25 mL) peanut oil

2 tbsp (25 mL) peanut oil

1 quantity Mekong Curry Paste

9 oz (250 g) vegetable marrow (prepared
  weight), peeled, seeded, and cut into
  1-in (2.5-cm) pieces

2 tbsp (25 mL) fish sauce

1 tbsp (15 mL) lemon juice

1 tsp (5 mL) soft brown sugar

1 tsp (5 mL) fresh lemongrass purée

1¼ cups (350 mL) coconut milk

1 lb 2 oz (500 g) large raw shrimp,
  peeled and deveined

GARNISH WITH

Finely chopped red onion

1 green chile, seeded and finely chopped

Mekong curry paste

Cambodian cuisine is often described as similar to the food of its Thai and Laotian neighbors but with a hint of Chinese stirred in for good measure. Rice is the country's staple food, cooked without salt and usually eaten at every meal with a fish, curry, or vegetable accompaniment. Most dishes are cooked in a wok and served as soon as they are ready.

As with its neighbors Vietnam, Laos, Myanmar (Burma) and Thailand, Cambodia has its own version of fish sauce called nguoc mam, which is an integral part of the country's cuisine. Both the Mekong River and the sea produce a plentiful supply of fish and shellfish which are used to make curries such as this.

Place all the ingredients in a food processor and blend to a paste, stopping periodically to push down the contents of the bowl as they spread up the sides.

Kari bonkong trasak SHRIMP AND MARROW CURRY

1 Heat the oil in a wok with a lid or a large skillet. Add the curry paste and fry over very low heat for 10 minutes or until softened and golden brown.

2 Add the marrow, fish sauce, lemon juice, sugar, lemongrass purée, and coconut milk. Cover the pan and simmer for 5 minutes.

3 Stir in the shrimp, uncover the pan, and cook for a further 5 minutes until the shrimp turn pink and the marrow is tender.

4 Garnish with chopped red onion and green chile. Serve with boiled rice.

SERVES 4

VARIATIONS This curry can also be made with chicken or cubes of a firm white fish.

Red chile, nut, and onion paste

2 large red chiles, seeded and chopped, or
   1 to 2 tsp (5 to 10 mL) sambal oelek
2 large red onions, peeled and chopped
1-in (2.5-cm) piece galangal or gingerroot,
   peeled and chopped
4 cloves garlic, peeled and chopped
½ tsp (2 mL) blachan (shrimp paste)
1 tsp (5 mL) turmeric
½ cup (125 mL) raw cashews, blanched
   almonds or Brazil nuts
2 tbsp (25 mL) peanut or vegetable oil

Candlenuts, known as buah keras in Malaysia, would be added to a curry paste like this to thicken it and add texture to the finished sauce. They are not readily available in the West but unsalted raw cashews, blanched almonds, or Brazil nuts could be substituted. This paste uses a moderate amount of chiles but add more if you wish.

Sambal refers to the spicy chile paste used as the basis for this dish. Many Malaysian curries are described as "asam," which means they include tamarind pulp for a distinctive sour flavor but this recipe uses the pungent blachan (shrimp paste) in the spice paste instead. Serve with boiled rice or noodles.

Blend the ingredients to a paste in a food processor.

Sambal udang SHRIMP SAMBAL

2 tbsp (25 mL) peanut or vegetable oil
1 quantity Red Chile, Nut, and
   Onion Paste
1 tbsp (15 mL) soft brown sugar
¾ cup (200 mL) thick coconut milk
Juice of 2 limes
1½ lb (675 g) medium-sized raw shrimp,
   peeled and heads removed

1 Heat the oil in a large skillet, add the paste, and cook gently for 10 to 15 minutes until tender and aromatic.
2 Add the sugar, coconut milk, and lime juice and bring to simmering point.
3 Add the shrimp and cook gently for 5 minutes until they turn opaque.
SERVES 4

VARIATIONS Use cubes of white fish or baby squid instead of shrimp. Alternatively, use a mixture of fish and shellfish.

Chile spice paste

The Serani (or Eurasian) people of Malaysia are the descendants of the original Portuguese, Dutch and British colonialists who settled in Melaka in the early 18th century. They are famous for their superb cooking, and today their cuisine is an exotic blend of Portuguese piri piri (hot pepper sauce), Dutch East Indian spice mixes, and even English roast meats and pies.

When frying the eggplants in this recipe, use a heavy non-stick skillet and keep the heat high or the eggplants will absorb too much oil, which will leak out again after cooking making the dish very greasy.

1 Place the chiles in a bowl and pour over boiling water to cover. Soak for 15 minutes until soft, then drain and seed.
2 Grind the chiles, shallots, garlic, cumin and fennel seeds, and gingerroot in a blender or spice grinder, adding enough oil to make a smooth paste. Add the paprika and mix well.

4 large dried chiles
6 shallots, peeled
3 cloves garlic, peeled
1½ tsp (7 mL) cumin seeds
½ tsp (2 mL) fennel seeds
1-in (2.5-cm) piece gingerroot, peeled and sliced
1 tbsp (15 mL) vegetable oil
1 tsp (5 mL) paprika

Brinjal pacheree EGGPLANTS WITH SPICY SAUCE

1 Mix the turmeric and salt together and dust over the eggplant chunks. Set aside for 10 minutes.
2 Heat half the oil in a heavy non-stick skillet. Fry the eggplant over high heat until browned. Remove from the skillet and set aside.
3 Add the remaining oil to the skillet, lower the heat to medium, and fry the spice paste for 6 to 7 minutes until fragrant and the oil separates out. Add the water, vinegar and sugar and stir well.
4 Stir the eggplant back into the skillet, cover and simmer for 10 minutes, stirring occasionally. **SERVES 4 AS A VEGETABLE ACCOMPANIMENT**

1 tsp (5 mL) turmeric
½ tsp (2 mL) salt
1 large eggplant, cut into small chunks
2 tbsp (25 mL) vegetable oil
1 quantity Chile Spice Paste
3 tbsp (45 mL) water
2 tbsp (25 mL) rice vinegar
2 tsp (10 mL) sugar

VARIATIONS Other vegetables, such as a mixture of sweet potatoes, zucchini and carrots, can be cooked in this way. Cut the potatoes and carrots into chunks and parboil for 5 minutes first. Brown the vegetables lightly in the oil, adding the turmeric and salt to the pan.

Curry devil spice mix

4 cloves garlic, peeled

1-in (2.5-cm) piece gingerroot,
    peeled and sliced

6 shallots or button onions, peeled

2 tsp (10 mL) mustard seeds

1 stalk lemongrass, chopped

1 tbsp (15 mL) vegetable oil

2 tbsp (25 mL) chili powder or to taste

1 tbsp (15 mL) turmeric

As its name suggests, a Malay Devil Curry is a racy blend of culinary fire due to the large numbers of chiles used in the spice mix. A close relative of a Goan Vindaloo, it is traditionally cooked on Boxing Day to use up leftover meat and these days can include anything from ham hocks and bacon bones to roast pork, chicken, and even sausages. A typical spice mix can use up to 30 dried chiles, which are soaked and then ground with other ingredients. This version uses dried chili powder and is much kinder to delicate Western palates—but you may increase the chili powder if you wish.

A relatively small number of Serani or Eurasian recipes are found in Malaysian cookbooks as generations of mothers have handed recipes down to their daughters, who then add their own personal stamp but guard them against the prying eyes of outsiders. Like much of their cuisine, Serani curries are adaptions of Indian and Malay dishes, spiced up with fresh or dried chiles and given a sour piquancy with the addition of vinegar or tamarind.

Blend the garlic, ginger, onions, mustard seeds, and lemongrass together with the oil in a spice grinder or food processor to make a smooth paste. Stir in the chili powder and turmeric.

Devil pork curry

2 tbsp (25 mL) vegetable oil

1 quantity Curry Devil Spice Mix

6 shallots, peeled and sliced

1 large carrot, peeled and sliced

4 medium-sized potatoes, peeled and
    cut into quarters

1.2 lb (500 g) lean pork, cubed

1 zucchini, sliced

1¼ cups (300 mL) chicken stock

1 tsp (5 mL) vinegar

GARNISH WITH

2 tbsp (25 mL) vegetable oil

1 large onion, peeled and thinly sliced

2 cloves garlic, peeled and thinly sliced

1 red chile, seeded and thinly sliced
    lengthwise

1 Heat the oil in a large pan and add the spice mix. Fry for 6 to 7 minutes over medium heat, stirring regularly. When the oil separates out, add the shallots, carrots and potatoes and fry for 5 minutes, stirring frequently.
2 Add the pork and zucchini and pour in the stock. Bring to a boil, cover, and simmer for 30 minutes. Add the vinegar and cook for a further 10 minutes or until the potatoes and carrots are tender.
3 When the curry is nearly ready, make the garnish. Heat the oil in a pan and fry the onion until soft. Add the garlic and chile and fry for 5 minutes until the onion and garlic are golden brown. Serve the curry with rice, and sprinkle with the garnish. **SERVES 4**

VARIATIONS Use cubed chicken or a lean, tender cut of beef instead of the pork.

8 Soups, broths, and stocks

Well-flavored broths and stocks are an essential ingredient in many Asian dishes. They are particularly important in China and Japan where an aromatic chicken broth or dashi stock will form the basis of soups served as part of a meal. In Thailand, too, light soups of fresh vegetables and herbs are drunk along with other dishes, rather than served as an appetizer or separate course, and provide a palate-cleansing contrast to more robust textures and flavors. A good beef stock defines the hearty Pho Bo soup, sold as street food all over Vietnam. In the north, warming spices like ginger and cinnamon flavor the broth but farther south, as the climate heats up, fiery chiles are added to cool the body down.

Dashi

The light, basic stock that is such a feature of Japanese cuisine. Subtly flavored with konbu (dried kelp) and bonito flakes, it is used for soups, dipping sauces and the one-pot dish Shabu-shabu, which is Japan's version of the Chinese Steamboat (see page 118).

Japanese soups are similar to consommé—clear and designed to cleanse the palate between more strongly flavored courses. The small shimeji mushrooms used in this soup have a nutty flavor and firm texture but shiitake, nameko, or enoki mushrooms may also be used. Wakame seaweed or spinach would probably be used in Japan in place of mushrooms but for the Western palate, mushrooms add a pleasant texture and flavor.

½-in (1-cm) strip dried kelp
5 cups (1.2 L) cold water
2 tbsp (25 mL) dried bonito flakes

1 Wipe the kelp with a damp cloth and cut into three or four pieces.
2 Place the kelp in a large saucepan with the water and bring slowly to a boil. As the water comes up to a boil, remove the kelp with a pair of spaghetti tongs or chopsticks and discard.
3 Sprinkle in the bonito flakes and remove the pan from the heat. As soon as the flakes start to sink, strain the stock through a fine sieve, discarding the flakes.

Tofu no miso shiru MISO SOUP WITH BEAN CURD

1 Put the Dashi in a saucepan and bring to a simmer. Add the miso, stirring until dissolved.
2 Add the mushrooms and tofu and simmer for 2 to 3 minutes without allowing the soup to boil.
3 Ladle into soup bowls and garnish each serving with a few fine shreds of scallion. **SERVES 4**

1 quantity Dashi
¼ cup (50 mL) aka (brown or red) miso
1½ oz (40 g) shimeji mushrooms, trimmed and rinsed
5 oz (150 g) silken tofu, cut into small cubes
4 scallions, finely shredded

VARIATIONS Other vegetables such as finely sliced carrot, white radish or bamboo shoots may be added to the dashi. For a more filling soup, add small pieces of shredded chicken, shrimp, and rice or soba (buckwheat noodles).

Chicken, soy, and ginger broth

5 cups (1.2 L) good-quality chicken stock
  or Chinese Chicken Broth (see page 118)
1-in (2.5-cm) piece gingerroot,
  peeled and grated
2 tbsp (25 mL) light soy sauce
1 tbsp (15 mL) rice wine or dry sherry
1 tsp (5 mL) sugar
Salt and pepper

Chinese soups are lighter and much less substantial than many Western chowders or cream soups and are drunk during the meal between helpings of more solid foods. Usually based on a clear broth, they include small pieces of meat, vegetables or seafood.

Canned or frozen corn may be used for this soup. Add it first to the stock and, if the corn is frozen, allow the stock to come back to a simmer before you add the other ingredients.

Heat the stock in a large saucepan with the gingerroot, soy sauce, rice wine or sherry, sugar, and seasoning until it comes to a boil.

Hai yook dahn gung   CORN, CRABMEAT, AND CHICKEN SOUP

2 tsp (10 mL) cornstarch
1 quantity Chicken, Soy, and Ginger Broth
7 oz (200 g) canned or frozen corn kernels
1 boneless chicken breast, skinned and
  cut into small pieces
9 oz (250 g) white crabmeat, coarsely
  flaked
2 eggs, lightly beaten
2 scallions, trimmed and finely sliced

1 Mix the cornstarch with 1 tablespoon water until smooth.
In a large saucepan, heat the broth until simmering. Stir in the cornstarch mixture until the broth thickens a little. Stir in the corn and chicken and simmer for 5 minutes.
2 Add the crabmeat. Slowly pour the beaten eggs down the tines of a fork, in as thin a stream as possible, trailing the fork over the surface of the soup. When the eggs have set in thin strings, stir the soup to evenly distribute them.
3 Spoon into soup bowls and sprinkle with the scallions. Serve at once.
SERVES 4

VARIATIONS In place of the chicken, add the same quantity of small peeled shrimp to the soup with the crabmeat.

Chicken, rice wine, and fresh cilantro broth

Use the basic Chinese Chicken Broth (see page 118) for this recipe or buy good-quality ready-prepared fresh stock, stock powder or cubes. Soup stalls are a common sight in Chinese markets, with wonton soup one of the most popular. In China, soups are eaten as a sustaining snack or a light meal with another dish, rather than being served as a separate course as they often are in the West.

The Cantonese "wonton" translates as "a swallowed cloud." In the rest of China these small dumplings are known as "huntun," a Mandarin word derived from "hundun" or "chaos," which signifies the dawn of mankind in Chinese folklore and legend. In Beijing and northern China, huntun are always eaten on 22 December, the first day of winter, when ancestors are traditionally remembered.

In a large saucepan, bring the broth or stock to a boil. Add the soy sauce and rice wine. Stir in the fresh cilantro and simmer for 5 minutes, then set aside to cool.

5 cups (1.2 L) Chinese Chicken Broth or good-quality chicken stock

2 tbsp (25 mL) light soy sauce

2 tbsp (25 mL) rice wine or dry sherry

2 tbsp (25 mL) finely chopped fresh cilantro

Wonton soup

1 Mix together the pork, shiitake mushrooms, scallions, ginger purée, sesame oil, soy sauce, and seasoning.

2 Spoon a little of the pork mixture onto the center of one wonton wrapper, dampen the edges and lift the sides up around the filling. Press together at the top to make a small "money bag." Repeat with the remaining wrappers and filling.

3 Soak the dried mushrooms in boiling water for 30 minutes until tender. Bring the broth to a boil in a large saucepan. Drain the dried mushrooms and strain the soaking liquid into the broth. Add the soaked mushrooms and bok choy and drop in the wontons one by one. Simmer gently for 10 minutes. Serve sprinkled with the sliced scallions. **SERVES 4**

VARIATIONS Ground chicken or coarsely chopped shrimp can be used in the wonton filling instead of pork.

6 oz (175 g) ground pork

4 oz (100 g) shiitake mushrooms, finely chopped

2 scallions, trimmed and finely chopped

½ tsp (2 mL) fresh ginger purée

Few drops sesame oil

1 tbsp (15 mL) light soy sauce

Salt and pepper

20 wonton wrappers

1½ oz (40 g) dried Chinese mushrooms

1 quantity Chicken, Rice Wine, and Fresh Cilantro Broth

1 head bok choy, shredded

GARNISH WITH

4 scallions, thinly sliced

4½ cups (1 L) water

5 tbsp (65 mL) Chinese black tea leaves

3 tbsp (45 mL) dark soy sauce

1 tsp (5 mL) freshly ground Szechwan
   pepper

1 tsp (5 mL) salt

1 tbsp (15 mL) Chinese 5-spice powder

6 eggs

1 quantity hot Black Tea Broth

Black tea broth

Tea has been drunk in China since at least the 6th century B.C. and there are tea plantations all over the southern part of the country. Different styles of tea refer to their infusion rather than the color of their leaves. To make this broth you will need a Chinese black tea such as Keemun or Lapsang Souchong rather than one of the "green" varieties.

The Chinese rarely eat egg dishes in the way Westerners might serve an omelet or frittata but they do have a unique way of cooking eggs by steeping them in a dark brew of black tea, spices, and soy sauce. The marbled pattern is achieved by carefully crazing the shells of the cooked eggs by tapping them all over with a spoon.

Put the ingredients in a saucepan and bring to a simmering.

Cha yip dahn MARBLED TEA EGGS

1 Place the eggs in a saucepan, cover with cold water, and bring slowly to a boil. Simmer for 7 minutes, then drain and cool the eggs in a bowl of cold water for 10 minutes, changing the water once or twice if it becomes warm. Drain and tap the eggshells all over with a teaspoon to create a fine network of cracks.

2 Bring the Black Tea Broth to a simmer, add the cracked eggs, making sure they are submerged, and simmer for 15 minutes.

3 Remove the saucepan from the heat and allow the eggs to cool in the broth. Transfer the broth and eggs to a bowl. Cover, and chill in the refrigerator for several hours or overnight.

4 When ready to serve, drain the eggs and carefully peel away the shells. Serve the eggs cut into halves or wedges as a garnish for hors d'oeuvres and cold dishes, or with a dipping sauce as an appetizer. **SERVES 6**

VARIATION Quails' eggs can be marbled in the same way to make an attractive garnish for an appetizer or to serve as an hors d'oeuvre with drinks. Reduce the initial boiling time to 3 minutes and the time in the broth to 10 minutes.

Spicy beef stock

5 cups (1.2 L) beef stock or canned
   consommé
2 cloves garlic, peeled and finely sliced
1-in (2.5-cm) piece gingerroot, peeled and
   cut into matchsticks
1 star anise
1 cinnamon stick
Salt and pepper

The two most common sights on a busy Vietnamese street are bicycles and pho (pronounced "fer"), food stalls that sell steaming bowls of rice noodle and beef soup, Vietnam's version of comfort food. The stock base is made from beef shin bones and meat scraps that are slowly simmered to make a clear rich stock. Herbs, spices, and garlic are then added according to each cook's own favorite blend. Because the stock can take up to a day to prepare, substituting a good-quality ready-made beef stock or consommé is usually more practical for the home cook.

Who makes the definitive "pho" has long been the subject of intense rivalry between Hanoi and Saigon. The north Vietnamese say their city is the only place to enjoy the true "Hanoi beef soup," while the south proclaim their version to be sweeter and spicier and therefore superior. When a customer stops by, the pho stall holder is ready with precooked rice noodles, wafer-thin slices of raw beef, shredded scallions, and gingerroot. The noodles are swiftly reheated, placed in a bowl, and beef and vegetables laid on top. Finally the hot stock is ladled in from a steaming cauldron alongside. Finishing touches are left to the customer's personal taste, with a selection of condiments such as chile or fish sauce, lime wedges, or other flavorings from the selection of garnishes laid out nearby.

In a large saucepan, bring the stock or consommé to a boil. Add the garlic, gingerroot, star anise, cinnamon, and seasoning and simmer gently for 15 minutes. Remove from the heat, cover, and allow to cool, then strain.

Pho bo ha noi BEEF AND RICE NOODLE SOUP

1 quantity Spicy Beef Stock
1 lb 2 oz (500 g) cooked flat rice noodles
12 oz (350 g) rump or sirloin steak, sliced
   as thinly as possible
4 scallions, finely sliced
1 tsp (5 mL) finely grated gingerroot
2 tbsp (25 mL) chopped fresh cilantro
2 tbsp (25 mL) chopped mint

SERVE WITH

Lime wedges
4 oz (100 g) bean sprouts
Chile sauce
Fish sauce

1 Bring the stock to a boil. Have the rice noodles freshly cooked or if you have precooked them, reheat by immersing briefly in a saucepan of boiling water.
2 Drain the noodles and divide into four deep soup bowls. Add the slices of steak, scallions, gingerroot, fresh cilantro and mint, and pour over the boiling stock.
3 Serve with lime wedges, bean sprouts, chile sauce, and fish sauce for diners to add to the soup as they wish. SERVES 4

VARIATIONS If Asian basil, which has purple stalks and a mild aniseed scent, is available it can replace the mint.

Chicken, lemongrass, and lime leaf stock

Tom Yum is probably Thailand's most famous soup and like so many of the country's dishes its success depends on combining a few simple ingredients for maximum effect. The stock for the soup is made by boiling whole raw shrimp in water flavored with lemongrass and lime leaves. The shrimp are then drained and peeled and their heads and shells added to the pot for extra flavor. Since most of us are unable to buy raw shrimp as fresh and flavorful as those available to Thai cooks, this recipe is based on a well-flavored chicken stock, with shrimp added later when it is made into a soup.

As with other Asian soups, in Thai homes Tom yum goong would be served with a selection of dishes plus rice as a main meal rather than as a first course. If you can find Thai basil, garnish the soup with some torn leaves; if not, use fresh cilantro.

Bring the stock to a boil in a large saucepan. Add the lemongrass and galangal purées and lime leaves and simmer for 5 minutes. Add the nam pla, lime juice, and sliced chiles, adding extra chiles according to taste.

Tom yum goong HOT AND SOUR SOUP

1 Bring the stock to a boil in a large saucepan and add the chicken, snow peas, and scallions. Simmer for 3 minutes.
2 Add the shrimp and simmer for a further 2 minutes or until the shrimp turn pink. Spoon into soup bowls and garnish with torn Thai basil leaves or fresh cilantro leaves. **SERVES 4**

VARIATION Add mushrooms to the soup with the chicken. Choose an Oriental variety such as shiitake or canned straw mushrooms, and halve or quarter so they sit in the bowl of a spoon comfortably.

3 cups (700 mL) light, well-flavored chicken stock
1 tsp (5 mL) fresh lemongrass purée
1 tsp (5 mL) galangal purée
2 kaffir lime leaves, sliced wafer-thin
3 tbsp (45 mL) nam pla (Thai fish sauce)
4 tbsp (50 mL) lime juice
2 medium red chiles or more to taste, seeded and thinly sliced

1 quantity Chicken, Lemongrass, and Lime Leaf Stock
1 chicken breast, skinned and cut into small pieces
12 snow peas, halved
2 scallions, thinly sliced on the diagonal
8 large shrimp, peeled and deveined

GARNISH WITH

Thai basil or fresh cilantro leaves

Chinese chicken broth

A good chicken broth forms the basis of many Chinese dishes, which rely on its delicate flavor to complement other ingredients. Stock made from powder or cubes can be substituted in recipes but the finished dish will not have such a fine flavor. Unused stock can be frozen for use in other recipes, as can any uncooked bones and chicken trimmings you may want to save until you have enough to make the stock.

Also called a Mongolian Fire Pot or Hot Pot, this eastern-style fondue is popular all round the Mekong Delta. The special cooking pot can be found in Chinese food stores. Traditional pots are fired with charcoal, which is placed down the center chimney, but modern pots are usually electric. The pot is set in the middle of the table, filled with the hot stock. Guests are given a selection of fish, seafood, meat, and vegetables which they drop into the simmering stock using chopsticks. Each diner has a small wire strainer for lifting out the cooked food into individual bowls, before dipping it in sauces such as soy, chile and hoi sin. When all the food has been eaten, the stock, which has absorbed lots of delicious new flavors, is served as a soup to complete the meal.

4 lb (1.8 kg) raw chicken carcasses, wings, thighs or other chicken pieces

3 quarts (3.4 L) cold water

1 medium onion, peeled and sliced

2-in (5-cm) piece gingerroot, peeled and sliced

4 cloves garlic, unpeeled and halved

1 stick celery, sliced

1 Put all the chicken bones and pieces in a large, tall, heavy saucepan and pour over the water to cover. Add the onion, ginger, garlic, and celery and bring slowly to a simmer.

2 With a slotted spoon, skim off any scum as it rises to the surface and continue doing this until the stock is clear.

3 Simmer over low heat for 3 to 4 hours, skimming as necessary. Do not allow the stock to boil or it will evaporate too quickly and become cloudy. Strain the stock through cheesecloth or a fine sieve and allow to cool. Chill for several hours, then lift off or blot any fat that has formed on the surface.

Steamboat

9 oz (250 g) fillet steak

9 oz (250 g) pork tenderloin

2 chicken breasts

9 oz (250 g) medium-sized raw shrimp

9 oz (250 g) monkfish or other firm white fish

9 oz (250 g) firm tofu

2 lb (900 g) mixed vegetables, e.g. carrots, snow peas, baby corn, Chinese mushrooms

¼ head bok choy

9 oz (250 g) green lip mussels, on the half shell

6 oz (175 g) rice or egg noodles, cooked

1 quantity Chinese Chicken Broth

1 Wrap the steak and pork separately in plastic wrap and freeze for 1 hour until firm. Unwrap and cut into ⅛-in (3-mm) slices using a sharp knife or cleaver.

2 Slice the chicken into thin strips across the grain of the meat. Peel the shrimp, removing the heads and tails. Cut the fish into small cubes or slices. Cut the tofu into cubes.

3 Prepare the vegetables and slice, halve or chop into bite-sized pieces as necessary. Shred the bok choy.

4 To serve, arrange the meat, chicken, fish, vegetables, shellfish, and noodles on large plates.

5 Place the hot pot in the center of the table on a heatproof stand and heat according to the manufacturer's instructions. Bring the broth to a boil and pour into the pot, topping up the pot during the meal as required. **SERVES 8**

Spicy coconut broth

Coconut milk is used as the base for many sauces and soups in the Malay Peninsula. Locals will make a broth similar to this and add chicken, bean curd, seafood, vegetables, flat rice noodles, or whatever else takes their fancy, to create one of the many variations of this popular seafood dish.

Locals would probably eat Laksa as a mid-morning snack but we would probably enjoy it more as a lunch or supper dish. If flat rice noodles are hard to find, use dried rice vermicelli or fine egg noodles, soaked according to the package instructions.

1 Heat the oil in a wok or large skillet and fry the onion over gentle heat until softened, stirring frequently. Add the ground almonds, garlic, lemongrass purée, shrimp paste, turmeric, chiles, ground cumin, and ground coriander and cook gently for 5 minutes.
2 Stir in the coconut milk and sugar. Season to taste.

2 tbsp (25 mL) vegetable oil

1 medium onion, peeled and finely sliced

½ cup (125 ml) ground almonds

3 cloves garlic, peeled and chopped

1 tsp (5 mL) fresh lemongrass purée

½ tsp (2 mL) shrimp paste

1 tsp (5 mL) turmeric

2 red chiles, seeded and chopped

2 tsp (10 mL) ground cumin

2 tsp (10 mL) ground coriander

4½ cups (1 L) coconut milk

1 tbsp (15 mL) palm sugar or
   soft brown sugar

Salt and pepper

Laksa lemak SEAFOOD LAKSA

1 In a wok or large saucepan, slowly bring the broth to a simmer. Stir in the shrimp and squid.
2 Meanwhile, in a large skillet, heat the oil and stir-fry the snow peas and bean sprouts for 2 to 3 minutes until they start to soften. Cook or soak the noodles according to the package instructions.
3 Drain the noodles and divide into four serving bowls. Spoon the snow peas and bean sprouts on top and sprinkle over the fresh cilantro. Ladle the hot coconut broth and seafood into the bowls and sprinkle with the chile and scallions. Serve at once with shrimp crackers. **SERVES 4**

VARIATION Instead of adding seafood to the broth, add two cooked chopped chicken breasts and cubes of firm tofu fried in 2 tablespoons hot oil until golden.

1 quantity Spicy Coconut Broth

12 oz (350 g) medium-sized raw
   shrimp, peeled

9 oz (250 g) squid, cut into rings or
   small pieces if large

2 tbsp (25 mL) vegetable oil

6 oz (175 g) snow peas, halved
   (diagonally across pod)

4 oz (100 g) bean sprouts

8 oz (225 g) flat rice noodles

2 tbsp (25 mL) chopped fresh cilantro

GARNISH WITH

1 red chile, seeded and finely sliced

2 scallions, finely shredded

1 tbsp (15 mL) peanut oil

1-in (2.5-cm) piece gingerroot,
   peeled and grated

2 cloves garlic, peeled and finely chopped

1 tbsp (15 mL) Thai red curry paste
   (see page 98)

2 medium-sized tomatoes, peeled,
   seeded, and diced

¾ cup (200 mL) coconut cream or
   thick coconut milk

3 cups (700 mL) chicken stock

2 tbsp (25 mL) nam pla (Thai fish sauce)

Juice of 1 lime

1 tsp (5 mL) soft brown sugar

2 tbsp (25 mL) peanut oil

3 boneless chicken breasts, cut into
   bite-sized pieces

6 oz (175 g) medium-sized raw shrimp,
   peeled and coarsely chopped

1 quantity Coconut, Red Curry, and
   Chicken Broth

6 oz (175 g) medium dried egg noodles,
   broken into short lengths

GARNISH WITH

Fresh cilantro leaves

Coconut, red curry, and chicken broth

Coconuts grow in abundance in southern Thailand, so their milk is often added to broths and stocks to make soup. Chiles are added to counteract the sweetness of the coconut, but only sparingly so they do not overpower other, more subtle ingredients.

The soup base can be made ahead and then allowed to stand for an hour so the flavors can infuse. When ready to serve, reheat gently without allowing the soup to boil.

1 Heat the oil in a large skillet or wok, add the gingerroot, garlic, and curry paste and fry over gentle heat for 3 minutes.

2 Stir in the tomatoes and coconut cream or milk and cook for 2 minutes, then add the stock, fish sauce, lime juice, and sugar. Simmer over low heat for 10 minutes.

Tom yum gai CHICKEN AND SEAFOOD SOUP

1 Heat the oil in a wok or large skillet and stir-fry the chicken over brisk heat for 5 minutes until lightly browned. Drain from the pan and set aside.

2 Add the shrimp to the pan and stir-fry until they turn pink. Drain and set aside.

3 Heat the broth until simmering, add the chicken and shrimp and keep over very low heat while you cook the noodles.

4 Cook the noodles in a pan of boiling water for 4 minutes or until tender. Drain and divide into four soup plates or bowls. Spoon the soup over the noodles and garnish with fresh cilantro leaves. **SERVES 4**

VARIATION For a vegetarian soup, replace the chicken and shrimp with a selection of stir-fried shredded vegetables such as zucchini, bell peppers, carrots, bean sprouts and mushrooms.

9 Sauces as accompaniments

From the piquant sweet and sour sauce served with shrimp in China to the
aromatic Vietnamese galangal and soy sauce that is spooned over fish, sauces
as accompaniments to meat, fish, seafood or vegetables play an
important part in Asian cuisines. Certain favorite ingredients recur
in similar sauces all over the region. The satay peanut sauce to
accompany Malaysian satays becomes a coating sauce for
Bang bang chicken in China, while in Indonesia it is
spooned over steamed vegetables as a dressing for the
popular Gado-gado salad. Spring rolls too appear in
different guises across Asia. They can be fried or
steamed, wrapped in crisp bean curd jackets or
lacy rice pancakes, but all have a tangy
accompanying sauce either spooned over
them or served on the side.

1 medium onion, peeled and finely
   chopped

2 tbsp (25 mL) vegetable or peanut oil

2 cloves garlic, peeled and crushed

1 tsp (5 mL) sambal oelek

1 stock-cube-sized piece trassie (shrimp
   paste)

3 tbsp (45 mL) kecap manis (thick, dark
   soy sauce)

2 tbsp (25 mL) brown sugar

12 oz (350 g) crunchy peanut butter

Juice of 1½ limes

1¼ cups (300 mL) water

4 boneless chicken breasts, skinned

1 tsp (5 mL) salt

1-in (2.5-cm) piece gingerroot,
   peeled and grated

3 cloves garlic, peeled and minced

½ tsp (2 mL) ground cumin

2 tsp (10 mL) ground or puréed laos

2 tbsp (25 mL) brown sugar

Juice of ½ lime

1 tbsp (15 mL) ground coriander

2 tbsp (25 mL) kecap manis

2 tsp (10 mL) vegetable oil

Ground white pepper

Extra oil, for brushing

SERVE WITH

1 quantity Sate Peanut Sauce

Sate peanut sauce

The sauce best-known in the West to accompany satay and also to serve as a
dressing for the shredded Indonesian vegetable salad Gado-gado (see page 41). The
sauce can be kept refrigerated in a covered container for several weeks or it can be
frozen. Reheat when ready to serve, adding more water if it has become too thick.

In Indonesia, you will find satay made with ground beef, bone marrow and offal,
as well as with chicken. Offal is a great local favorite and might include tripe, heart,
and tongue. Soak the wooden skewers in cold water for 30 minutes before threading
the chicken on to them so they do not burn under the broiler.

Fry the onion in the oil until it is soft and golden brown. Add the remaining
ingredients, keeping the heat low and stirring constantly for a couple of
minutes until you have an evenly mixed sauce.

Sate ayam CHICKEN SATAY WITH PEANUT SAUCE

1 Cut the chicken into thin strips across the grain of the meat and spread
out in a shallow dish.
2 Pound the salt, ginger, and garlic together in a mortar and pestle to make
a paste and mix with the other ingredients, adding white pepper to taste.
Spoon the mixture over the chicken, cover, and allow to marinate overnight.
3 Drain the chicken and thread onto dampened wooden skewers. Brush with
oil and broil or barbecue for 5 minutes, turning over once or twice.
4 Serve hot with the warm peanut sauce. If you have made the sauce ahead
and it is too thick, stir in extra water to obtain the desired consistency.
SERVES 8

VARIATIONS Beef, lamb, pork, or other poultry are popular alternatives to chicken
when making satay.

Galangal and ginger sauce

Centuries of foreign occupation have seen Vietnamese cooking influenced by outside cuisines as diverse as Indian, Chinese and French, the latter in particular shaping the tastes and eating habits of local residents. Avocados, asparagus, tomatoes, and corn sit alongside durian and jackfruit in the markets, while lunch for an office worker might well be a paté-filled baguette and café au lait. Cream and other dairy products are also added to modern sauces and desserts, as in this delicately spiced sauce for fish.

If possible, use young, small spinach leaves for this dish. If only larger leaves are available, cut out any tough stalks before shredding the leaves. Spinach should only be cooked until the leaves have just wilted, so it retains all its flavor and color.

1 Heat the butter in a saucepan until foaming, add the shallots, and fry gently for 5 minutes. Stir in the galangal and ginger and cook for 2 minutes, then add the rice vinegar and sugar.

2 Blend the cornstarch with a little of the stock until smooth. Stir into the saucepan with the rest of the stock and bring slowly to a boil, stirring constantly. Lower the heat and simmer for 10 minutes, stirring occasionally. Stir in the fresh cilantro and crème fraîche and season with salt and pepper.

½ oz (15 g) butter

3 shallots, peeled and finely chopped

1 tsp (5 mL) fresh galangal purée

1 tsp (5 mL) fresh ginger purée

2 tbsp (25 mL) rice vinegar

1 tsp (5 mL) sugar

1 tbsp (15 mL) cornstarch

2½ cups (600 mL) fish stock

2 tbsp (25 mL) finely chopped fresh cilantro

4 tbsp (50 mL) crème fraîche

Salt and pepper

Ca chep kho rieng

BROILED CARP WITH GALANGAL AND GINGER SAUCE

1 Place the fish fillets in a dish. Mix together the oil, fish sauce, soy sauce, and rice vinegar, and pour over the fish. Set aside in a cool place for 2 hours.

2 Lift the fish from the marinade and broil for 2 to 3 minutes each side, depending on thickness, until cooked.

3 While the fish is cooking rinse the spinach leaves and cook in a large saucepan with just the rinsing water clinging to the leaves, until wilted. Gently reheat the sauce.

4 To serve, spoon the spinach onto individual serving plates and place the fish on top. Cover with some of the sauce and serve the remaining sauce separately in a jug. Garnish with Chinese chives and fine slices of red chile.

SERVES 4

Four 6-oz (175-g) whole carp or red snapper fillets

2 tbsp (25 mL) vegetable oil

2 tbsp (25 mL) fish sauce

2 tbsp (25 mL) soy sauce

1 tbsp (15 mL) rice vinegar

4 oz (100 g) fresh spinach leaves

1 quantity Galangal and Ginger Sauce

GARNISH WITH

Chinese chives and fine slices of red chile

VARIATIONS Other small whole fish such as trout or red mullet are used for this dish, or cod or salmon steaks, skinned or not, as you prefer.

Peanut and sesame sauce

5 tbsp (65 mL) crunchy peanut butter

½ tsp (2 mL) sweet chile sauce

1 tbsp (15 mL) dark soy sauce

¼ cup (100 mL) peanut oil

½ tsp (2 mL) sesame oil

Juice of 1 lime

Peanut traces dating from the third century B.C. have been unearthed in southeast China and today peanuts are one of the country's most important crops. Peanuts are cultivated in rotation with rice or wheat along the Yangtze and Yellow rivers and in the river valleys inland. They grow in pods which develop in clusters under the ground, giving them their alternative name, groundnuts.

Bang bang chicken is a Szechwan dish from western China, where it is known as Bon bon chicken after the stick (bon) that is used to pound the chicken and tenderize it.

Place the peanut butter, chile sauce, and soy sauce in a food processor and blend for a few seconds until combined. With the motor running, gradually drizzle the peanut oil down the feeder tube of the food processor. When all the peanut oil has been added, add the sesame oil and lime juice and blend until evenly mixed in.

Bang bang chicken

1 medium carrot, cut into matchsticks

4 scallions, thinly sliced

½ red onion, peeled and thinly sliced

1 lb (450 g) cooked chicken, skinned and
    thinly shredded

1 quantity Peanut and Sesame Sauce

GARNISH WITH

Lime wedges

1 tbsp (15 mL) black sesame seeds

1 Arrange a pile of carrot, scallions, and red onion slices in the center of four serving plates. Top with the chicken.
2 Thin the sauce with a little warm water to a coating consistency if necessary, and spoon over the chicken. Serve at once with lime wedges and sprinkled black sesame seeds. **SERVES 4 AS AN APPETIZER**

VARIATIONS Substitute turkey or lean roast pork for the chicken.

Hoi sin and ginger sauce

2 tsp (10 mL) peanut oil

1 tsp (5 mL) fresh ginger purée

2 cloves garlic, peeled and crushed

6 tbsp (75 mL) hoi sin sauce

3 tbsp (45 mL) rice wine or dry sherry

1 tbsp (15 mL) light soy sauce

Also known as Chinese barbecue sauce, hoi sin is commonly used as a glaze for spareribs or chicken wings or as a dip for spring rolls. Its sweet flavor goes very well with plainly broiled or fried food. Here it is spiked with ginger and rice wine to serve with seafood or fish.

For this dish, you need to fry the shrimp quickly in hot oil until only just done or they will toughen and become tasteless. The light cornstarch and egg white batter protects their delicate flesh from the hot oil.

Heat the oil in a pan, add the ginger purée and garlic, and fry gently for 2 minutes. Stir in the hoi sin, rice wine, and soy sauce until evenly blended.

Geung cao dai ha

FRIED SHRIMP WITH HOI SIN AND GINGER SAUCE

2 tsp (10 mL) cornstarch

½ tsp (2 mL) salt

1 egg white

1 lb 2 oz (500 g) raw jumbo shrimp, peeled and deveined

2 tbsp (25 mL) peanut oil, plus extra for deep-frying

1 medium-sized onion, peeled and sliced

1 red bell pepper, seeded and chopped

SERVE WITH

1 quantity Hoi Sin and Ginger Sauce and boiled rice

1 Whisk the cornstarch, salt, and egg white together in a bowl, add the shrimp, and stir until coated. Allow to stand for 1 hour.
2 Heat 2 tablespoons oil in a skillet, add the onion and bell pepper, and fry for 5 minutes, stirring frequently. Add the sauce and bring to a boil. Simmer over gentle heat while you cook the shrimp.
3 Heat oil for deep-frying in a wok, add half the shrimp, and fry for 3 to 4 minutes until just done. Drain on paper towels and fry the rest of the shrimp in the same way.
4 Serve the shrimp with the sauce spooned over them. Accompany with boiled rice. **SERVES 4**

VARIATION Substitute strips of white fish such as flounder or sole for the shrimp.

Lemon sauce

A Cantonese sauce popular in Hong Kong and western Chinese restaurants rather than in mainland China. The tangy sauce is clean and refreshing on the palate but its origins are unclear because while the sweet orange originated in China no one is certain where the lemon was discovered and, apart from its use in this sauce, it does not feature widely in Chinese cooking.

Some recipes for lemon chicken use a heavy egg batter to coat the chicken but this one, made with just flour and water, is lighter and better suited to the delicate citrus sauce. Serve the dish garnished with shredded scallions and accompany with egg-fried rice.

Mix the cornstarch with the lemon juice until smooth and add to a saucepan with the stock, honey, sugar, and gingerroot. Stir over low heat until the sauce comes to a boil and it clears and thickens. Simmer for 1 minute.

2 tbsp (25 mL) cornstarch
½ cup (125 mL) freshly squeezed
    lemon juice
1½ cups (350 mL) chicken stock
2 tbsp (25 mL) clear honey
4 tbsp (50 mL) soft light brown sugar
1 tbsp (15 mL) grated gingerroot

Ling moong gai LEMON CHICKEN

1 Sift the flour and soda into a bowl, add the water, and whisk to make a smooth batter. Allow to stand for 30 minutes.
2 Cut each chicken breast into 3 or 4 pieces.
3 Heat oil for deep-frying in a wok to 350°F (180°C). Dip the chicken pieces in the batter and deep-fry for 8 to 10 minutes until golden. Drain on paper towels and serve at once with the hot sauce spooned over them.
SERVES 4

VARIATION For a more substantial meal, stir-fry some mixed vegetables such as bell peppers, mushrooms, and baby corn in a little oil in the wok. Drain these when done and keep warm while you add extra oil and deep-fry the chicken. Mix the chicken and vegetables together before covering with the lemon sauce.

2 cups (450 mL) self-raising flour
Pinch baking soda
1¼ cups (300 mL) cold water
4 boneless chicken breasts, skinned
Oil for deep-frying

SERVE WITH

1 quantity Lemon Sauce

Soy, vinegar, and chile sauce

A simple sauce to serve with spring rolls. Older Nyonya women once believed that they could determine how experienced a cook was by the rhythm of pounding ingredients in a mortar and pestle, and in days gone by they used this as a yardstick for matchmaking.

Crisply fried spring rolls are popular all over Southeast Asia, turning up as lumpia in the Philippines, nem in north Vietnam, and cha gio in south Vietnam. The Chinese dubbed them "spring rolls" because they were originally eaten to celebrate their New Year, which in China marks the first day of spring.

2 cloves garlic, peeled and chopped

1-in (2.5-cm) piece gingerroot, peeled and chopped

1 tsp (5 mL) dark brown sugar

3 tbsp (45 mL) soy sauce

1 tbsp (15 mL) rice vinegar

1 red chile, seeded and chopped

1 tbsp (15 mL) coarsely chopped fresh cilantro leaves

1 Pound the garlic and ginger with a mortar and pestle to make a paste, or grate and mash together. Place in a small bowl and add the brown sugar, soy sauce, and rice vinegar. Set aside for at least 1 hour.

2 Just before serving, strain into a serving bowl and add the chile and cilantro.

Poh piah NYONYA SPRING ROLLS

8 oz (225 g) ground pork

8 oz (225 g) raw shrimp, shelled and chopped

½ red bell pepper, seeded and finely chopped

4 shallots, peeled and finely chopped

4 oz (100 g) shiitake mushrooms, chopped

4 oz (100 g) canned water chestnuts, chopped

1 tsp (5 mL) fresh ginger purée

1 tbsp (15 mL) rice vinegar

1 tbsp (15 mL) light soy sauce

2 tbsp (25 mL) peanut oil

6 Chinese cabbage leaves, tough center stalks removed

1 tbsp (15 mL) cornstarch

12 spring roll wrappers

Extra peanut oil for deep- or shallow-frying

SERVE WITH

1 quantity Soy, Vinegar, and Chile Sauce

1 In a bowl, mix together the ground pork, shrimp, red bell pepper, shallots, mushrooms, water chestnuts, ginger, vinegar, and soy sauce.

2 Heat 2 tablespoons peanut oil in a skillet, add the pork mixture, and fry for 5 minutes, stirring frequently. Allow to cool.

3 Divide each cabbage leaf in half across the center. In a small bowl, mix the cornstarch with 4 tablespoons cold water until smooth.

4 Place half a cabbage leaf on one spring roll wrapper and top with a tablespoon of the pork mixture. Brush the edges of the wrapper with the cornstarch mix and roll up around the filling, tucking in the sides and pressing the brushed edges together to seal. Repeat with the remaining wrappers.

5 Deep- or shallow-fry the spring rolls in hot oil until golden brown all over. Drain on paper towels and serve hot with the Soy, Vinegar, and Chile Sauce spooned over them. **SERVES 4**

VARIATIONS Spring roll fillings can be varied to use up practically any leftover meat and vegetables. Cooked chopped chicken, pork, or ham could be added to fillings and vegetables such as diced carrots, bean sprouts and bamboo shoots.

Rice vinegar and Japanese soy sauce

3 tbsp (45 mL) rice vinegar

5 tbsp (65 mL) Japanese soy sauce

A tart sauce served to pour over the stuffed shiitake mushrooms served in Japan's yakitori bars (see page 75).

Just one of the hot snacks that can be enjoyed in Japan's "fast food" restaurants, where food is threaded onto skewers or stuffed with a spicy filling and roasted on a hot flat griddle. These shiitake mushrooms would probably be served in pairs in Japan, three and four being considered unlucky numbers. Choose medium-sized shiitake or cup mushrooms and pour the sauce over them just before serving. Hot English mustard or a Japanese wasabi paste could be served as an additional piquant relish. The mushroom stalks can be reserved for another recipe such as a soup or a stir-fry.

Mix the vinegar and soy sauce together.

Shiitake nikuzume CHICKEN-STUFFED MUSHROOMS

1 tsp (5 mL) fresh ginger purée

9 oz (250 g) ground chicken

Black pepper

1 small egg, lightly beaten

1 scallion, very finely chopped

16 to 20 shiitake or cup mushrooms, depending on size

2 tbsp (25 mL) vegetable oil

1 quantity Rice Vinegar and Japanese Soy Sauce

SERVE WITH

English mustard or wasabi paste

1 In a bowl, combine the ginger purée, ground chicken, pepper, beaten egg, and scallion. Mix well.
2 Remove the stalks from the mushrooms and rinse the caps. Pat dry with paper towels.
3 Spoon a little chicken mixture into each mushroom cap, pressing it down lightly and flattening the top.
4 Heat the oil in a large non-stick skillet over medium heat and add the mushrooms, chicken-side down. Cook for 5 minutes, then turn them over carefully. Place a lid over the pan and cook for a further 5 minutes.
5 Divide the mushrooms onto serving plates and drizzle with the sauce. Serve hot with mustard or wasabi paste on the side. **SERVES 4**

VARIATION Ground pork can be used instead of chicken.

10 Dessert sauces

The choice of desserts in Southeast Asia is far more limited than we are used to in the West. Sweetmeats, fritters or small cakes are generally served throughout the day as snacks, rather than as the final course of a formal meal. At home, Asian families will usually end a meal simply with fresh fruit, but restaurants are increasingly offering "desserts," most based on fresh coconut or fruits such as mangoes and lychees which are turned into jellies, sauces or custards. One meal that features desserts is "high tea," a specialty of Singapore's luxury hotels, where a mammoth buffet will be displayed including sweet dishes such as durian crème brûlée, chendol (a bright pyramid of crushed ice, threads of green bean flour jelly, coconut milk and colored palm sugar syrup), and small cakes filled with lotus seed paste.

Caramel toffee

1½ cups (350 mL) white sugar
¾ cup (175 mL) water
3 tbsp (45 mL) sesame seeds

Fruits such as apples and bananas fried in batter and coated in a shell of crisp gold toffee are a favorite Chinese dessert or snack. The toffee needs careful preparation: if the sugar boils before it has properly dissolved it will crystallize instead of becoming a smooth caramel. A wok is best for making the toffee, as it gives a more even heat distribution than a flat-bottomed saucepan.

Adding the batter-coated apple pieces one at a time to the hot oil prevents them from clumping together as they fry. When dipping the toffee apple pieces in the iced water, have extra ice cubes at hand because the hot toffee will quickly warm the water.

For instructions on making the toffee, see the recipe below.

Toffee apples

3 medium Granny Smith apples
1 cup (225 mL) all-purpose flour
About ¼ cup (100 mL) cold water
2 tsp (10 mL) vegetable oil
Vegetable oil for deep-frying
Sesame oil for greasing
1 quantity ingredients for Caramel Toffee
Ice cubes and cold water

1 Peel, core, and cut each apple into eight wedges.
2 Sift the flour into a bowl and stir in enough cold water to make a smooth batter. Finally stir in the 2 teaspoons of vegetable oil.
3 Heat oil for deep-frying in a wok to 375°F (190°C). Drop half a dozen pieces of apple into the batter, lift out one at a time with a slotted spoon, and place in the hot oil. Fry for 2 to 3 minutes until golden, remove with a slotted spoon, and drain on paper towels. Fry the rest of the apple pieces in the same way.
4 When all the apple wedges have been fried, drain the oil from the wok into another saucepan and set aside to cool before straining back into the bottle. Wipe the wok with paper towels.
5 Grease a large plate with the sesame oil and have ready a bowl filled with iced water and ice cubes.
6 To make the caramel toffee, heat the sugar and water gently in the wok until the sugar dissolves. Increase the heat and stir the syrup with a large metal spoon. After about 5 minutes of stirring, the syrup will become white and foamy but will become clear again after you have stirred for another few minutes. Continue boiling until the syrup caramelizes to a rich gold color. Remove from the heat and add the sesame seeds and apples, tossing lightly until coated.
7 Turn out immediately onto the greased plate and, using chopsticks, pick up the apple pieces one at a time and dip in the iced water so the toffee hardens. Serve at once. **SERVES 4**

VARIATIONS Banana and pineapple can also be prepared the same way.

Lime and brown sugar syrup

2½ cups (600 mL) water
Grated zest and juice of 2 limes
½ cup (125 mL) soft brown sugar

A tangy syrup that could be served with a tropical fresh fruit salad or spooned over pancakes or fritters.

In Indonesia "dadar" means any kind of flat food whether omelets, fritters, or French-style pancakes (or crêpes) such as these. The choice of desserts as we understand them in the West, is far more limited in Southeast Asian countries and when they are served coconut is likely to be one of the main flavorings. These pancakes are also popular in Thailand, where they are known as khan om krok.

Put the water, lime juice, and sugar in a heavy-based saucepan and heat gently until the sugar dissolves. Bring to a boil and simmer for 5 minutes then remove from the heat, stir in the lime zest, and allow to cool and infuse.

Dadar gulung COCONUT PANCAKES WITH FRESH FRUIT

Selection of tropical fruits, e.g.,
   mango, rambutan, guava, papaya,
   pineapple, banana (about 1½ lb
   [675 g] prepared weight)
1 quantity Lime and Brown Sugar Syrup

PANCAKES

3 oz (75 g) block creamed coconut
½ cup (125 mL) rice flour
2 medium eggs, beaten
4 tbsp (50 mL) white sugar
Red and blue food coloring
A little peanut oil for frying

SERVE WITH

Grated fresh coconut

1 Prepare the fruit as necessary, cut into bite-sized pieces and add to the cold syrup in the saucepan.
2 To make the pancakes, cut up the creamed coconut into small pieces and dissolve in ⅔ cup (150 mL) boiling water. Add ⅔ cup (150 mL) cold water, stir well, and allow to cool.
3 Place the flour in a bowl, make a well in the center and pour in the eggs. Add a little of the dissolved coconut and beat to mix with the flour. Stir in the remaining coconut and the sugar until smooth. Divide the batter equally into three bowls and color one mixture red and one blue with a few drops of coloring.
4 Heat an 8-in (20-cm) pancake skillet, lightly grease with a little oil, and pour in just enough batter from one of the bowls to coat the base of the pan in a thin layer. Cook for 2 minutes, then flip over and cook the other side for 2 minutes until lightly browned. Remove from the pan and keep warm while you cook the rest of the pancakes.
5 While the pancakes are cooking, heat the fruit in the syrup and simmer for 5 minutes. Serve the pancakes rolled with the fruit inside and the syrup spooned on top, or folded with the fruit and syrup on the side. Sprinkle with grated fresh coconut before serving.

SERVES 4

VARIATION Arranged on serving plates the different colored pancakes look attractive and make an unusual dessert. If preferred, however, leave the batter uncolored.

Egg and vanilla custard

A favorite Spanish dessert that Filipino cooks have adopted as their own is the caramel custard "flan." Recipes inevitably vary from cook to cook and in some the number of egg yolks added is rather more than we would consider healthy. This recipe hopefully strikes a happy balance between indulgence and health. In Asia, canned evaporated milk rather than fresh milk is also likely to be preferred, the cook claiming that the rich, creamy flavor of the finished dessert is much enhanced by its addition.

These caramel custards can be served in their dishes or turned out onto serving plates so the liquid caramel runs over them. A selection of fresh tropical fruits makes a good accompaniment or simply serve them on their own. On feast days or special occasions in the Philippines the custards are topped with slivers of macapuno, a local variety of sticky coconut.

3 large eggs
2 large egg yolks
½ cup (125 mL) white sugar
3 cups (700 mL) canned evaporated milk
Few drops vanilla extract

Beat the whole eggs and the yolks lightly together in a bowl, then whisk in the sugar. Heat the milk in a saucepan until bubbles appear across the surface. Pour the hot milk in a steady stream onto the egg mixture, whisking all the time until incorporated. Finally whisk in the vanilla.

Leche flan FILIPINO CARAMEL CUSTARD

1 Put the sugar and water in a small heavy-based saucepan and heat gently until the sugar dissolves. Bring to a boil and continue to boil hard until the syrup turns a rich golden brown. Pour into six ramekins or other heatproof molds, tilting them so the caramel coats the sides a little as well as the bases.
2 Preheat the oven to 325°F (170°C). Strain the custard into the molds and stand them in a roasting pan. Pour enough warm (not hot) water into the pan to come halfway up the sides of the molds. Bake in the oven for 45 minutes or until set.
3 Allow to cool before turning out onto dishes. **SERVES 6**

½ cup (125 mL) granulated sugar
⅔ cup (150 mL) water
1 quantity Egg and Vanilla Custard

VARIATIONS The custards can be flavored with a little grated orange or lime zest, rather than vanilla.

Mango coulis

Mangoes are one of the most widely used fruits in the Philippines and are particularly popular as a base for ice creams and other desserts. The dense, sweet mango flesh makes an excellent fruit coulis when the flavor is sharpened with apple and lime juice.

This fruity ice cream will set hard in the freezer, so to make it easier to serve, transfer the container to the refrigerator 30 minutes before serving to give it time to soften. Alternatively, freeze the ice cream in scoops on a baking sheet ready to serve.

Cut the mango flesh away from either side of the fibrous pit, peel, and place the chopped flesh in a food processor. Add the apple juice and lime juice and blend until smooth. The coulis should have a thick pouring consistency so if necessary, add a little more apple juice to achieve this.

1 large ripe mango
About ¾ cup (175 mL) apple juice
Juice of 1 lime

Pineapple and coconut ice cream

1 Whisk together the egg yolks, ½ cup (125 mL) of the white sugar, and the cornstarch in a bowl until creamy. Gradually whisk in the pineapple juice.
2 In a saucepan, heat the milk until just under boiling, pour slowly onto the egg mixture, and stir until blended. Pour back into the saucepan and stir over low heat until smooth and thickened.
3 Remove from the heat, transfer to a bowl, and sprinkle the remaining white sugar over the surface to prevent a skin forming. Allow to cool.
4 Stir in the coconut cream and whipped cream. Freeze in the bowl for 1 hour, then whisk to break up any ice crystals. Stir in the chopped pineapple, transfer to a freezer container, and freeze until firm.
5 Serve in scoops with the Mango Coulis drizzled over. Decorate with pineapple slices, lime slices, and a little finely grated lime zest. **SERVES 6**

3 large egg yolks
½ cup (125 mL) white sugar, plus
an extra 1 tbsp (15 mL)
1 tbsp (15 mL) cornstarch
⅔ cup (150 mL) unsweetened
pineapple juice
¾ cup (200 mL) milk
7-fl oz (200-mL) carton coconut cream
⅔ cup (150 mL) heavy cream, whipped
2 slices pineapple, chopped

SERVE WITH

1 quantity Mango Coulis
Pineapple slices
Lime slices and finely grated lime zest

VARIATIONS The coulis could be served over any ice cream or sorbet. It would go particularly well with a sharp fruit sorbet or a rich ice cream such as chocolate.

Coconut custard

In Thailand, coconut milk is often used to make a sweet, creamy custard, which is cooked in a double boiler and then a steamer to prevent bubbles forming in the custard. Canned Thai coconut milk is the right consistency for the recipe but because the cream tends to settle on the top, the milk needs a good stir or a quick whiz in a blender to restore its smooth texture. Take care not to allow the custard to boil or it will curdle. If this does happen, remove the saucepan from the heat and strain or process the custard in a blender until smooth again.

Most meals in Thailand end not with a dessert but with a platter of the many luscious fruits that grow all over the country. In this recipe, the Sankhaya (coconut custard) is served with a fresh fruit salad lightly spiced with cinnamon, star anise, and cloves.

2 large eggs, lightly beaten

¼ cup (50 mL) white sugar

1 cup (225 mL) thick canned coconut milk

Few drops vanilla extract

1 Whisk the eggs and sugar together until creamy then stir in the coconut milk until evenly blended.

2 Strain into a double boiler set over a pan of boiling water and cook gently, stirring constantly, until the mixture coats the back of a wooden spoon. Stir in the vanilla and pour the custard into four small bowls or ramekins. Cover lightly with foil and steam over just-simmering water for 15 minutes or until the custards are just set. Allow to cool.

Sankhaya COCONUT CUSTARD SERVED WITH SPICED FRUIT SALAD

1¼ cups (300mL) pineapple juice

2 star anise

1 cinnamon stick, broken into short lengths

4 cloves

1 mango, peeled and flesh sliced or chopped

½ papaya, peeled, seeded and chopped

1 slice pineapple, cut into small pieces

4 rambutans, peeled, pitted and halved

1 star fruit, sliced

Seeds from ½ pomegranate

SERVE WITH

4 Coconut Custards

1 Place the pineapple juice in a small pan, add the star anise, cinnamon, and cloves and bring to simmering point. Remove from the heat and set aside to cool.

2 Pile the prepared fruit in a serving bowl, pour the spiced juice over it, and chill until ready to serve.

3 Spoon the fruit salad onto serving plates, with the small bowls of custard on the side. **SERVES 4**

VARIATIONS A little grated fresh ginger, bruised lemongrass stalk, or split vanilla bean can be added to the pineapple juice. If rambutans are not available, lychees can be substituted. The custards can be dusted with a little ground cinnamon before serving, if liked.

Index